Engaging Alphabet Crafts and Activities for Preschoolers

To my daughter Abby,
Thank you for being my "artist in residence",
and helping to create all the projects in this book.
I love your creativity and eye for detail.
It is a blessing to watch you grow and learn each day.

- Mom

Getting Started With ABC FUN

The main activities in ABC FUN include removable templates for decorating each letter with a household item that starts with that letter, and creating an animal or object out of the letter. Each activity was designed to use typical household items to reinforce learning when your child uses that item in regular daily life. This will help your child to understand that letters make up a very important part of their life, and create opportunities to review the letter names and sounds as they recall how they used an apple to decorate the letter A or an old toothbrush to paint the letter T. Most of the items needed for the activities in this book should be easily found in your home, but I have provided a full list on the next page so you can see if there is anything you'll need to purchase before starting an activity.

Take your time.

Spend a few days on each letter. This will allow your child to have repeated exposure to the letter's name and sound as well as talk about different items they use and see on a daily basis that start with that letter.

Become familiar with the letter.

Take time to look at the letter. Look through books and magazines to identify objects that start with the letter your child is learning about. It may help to identify several objects on each page and then listen for the sound your child is learning. If possible, cut some of these items out and create a letter collage by gluing them to a paper with that letter written on it.

Learn on the go.

There is a food/snack section for each letter that includes a short list of food items that start with the letter being studied. It may be fun to go to the grocery store to look for something new to try that starts with each letter or possibly try a new recipe if your child likes to cook with you.

Make some noise.

An instrument is included for each letter. Look for pictures of these instruments or watch them being played online. You can even make a few of these instruments with simple items!

Most importantly, have FUN!

The idea for ABC FUN came from projects I did with my own daughter during the summer to help her learn the names and sounds of the ABC's. Many of the ideas came from my experience as a preschool teacher as well as some creative thinking and brainstorming. As you will see throughout ABC FUN there are many ways to engage your child in learning, but don't feel like you have to do it all. Just do what is interesting to your child. This book is intended to reach several age ranges, so everything might not be a fit for your child at their current age or learning stage.

Take pictures of your child creating their work. Display it around their room or slip their art into page protectors in a binder and create a book for them to look back through for many years to come. Remember, this is your child's project. Help them if they need help, but allow them to cut, paste, and paint as much on their own as possible. The projects don't have to be perfect; they just need to be your child's own work and cultivate their creativity.

Activity Supply List

You will need scissors, a glue stick, and construction paper for most projects in addition to the items listed below.

	Decorate the Letter:	Letter Craft:
A	apple, paint (1-2 colors), fork or popsicle stick	
B	bubbles, bubble wands, food coloring (2-4 colors), tape, medicine cups (one for each color)	
C	celery, ink pads	black crayon
D	dot painters, 2 dice (optional)	yellow craft feather (optional)
E	Easter eggs, paint (2-3 colors)	black or gray crayon
F	plastic forks, paint (2-3 colors)	white or blue paint, green paint or crayon
G	golfball, paint (green), casserole pan lined with foil or a disposable foil pan	dot paint, circle stickers, or craft pom poms (something to resemble gumballs)
H	highlighters (3-4 colors)	
I	ice cube tray, food coloring (3-5 colors), popsicle sticks, foil (optional), **24 hours to freeze**	red ribbon or yarn (a crayon will work as well), tape
J	jellybeans, toothpicks, bowl of water	ribbon or yarn (white, blue or pink), tape
K	keys, crayons	
L	leaves, paint (2-3 colors)	orange and black crayons, tape
M	marshmallows, paint (3-4 colors)	black crayon
N	spaghetti noodles (3-4, cooked), paint (3-4 colors)	blue craft feather (optional)
O	okra, ink pad	
P	pencils (2), paint (pink and purple)	
Q	glue stick, fabric scraps cut into 1in squares	stick on craft jewels (optional)
R	ruler, pencil, paint/ crayons/ or markers (red, orange, yellow, blue, indigo, and violet)	black crayon, cottonball (optional)
S	star stickers	
T	old toothbrush, paint (1-2 colors)	black crayon
U	crayons, tape	
V	toy car (vehicle), paint (violet)	green crayon
W	watercolors, paint brush	black crayon
X	black crayon	
Y	yarn, paint (yellow)	red and black crayons
Z	Ric-Rac ribbon (2-3 colors), liquid glue	black paint, marble, foil pan (all optional)

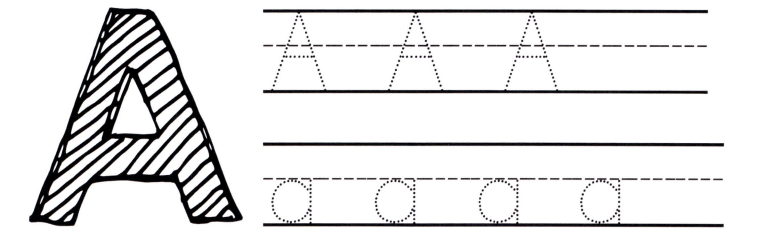

Letter Introduction:

Talk with your child about the letter "A" and the sounds that the letter makes (it says it's name "a" and "ah"). Help your child think of different objects that start with the letter A (alligator, ant, apple, astronaut, airplane, acorn). You could look through books, pointing out objects that start with A or cut pictures from magazines and make an "A collage" together.

Also talk about how the letter is formed. Have your child trace over the letters provided above with his/her finger and then with a pencil or crayon. Try to encourage proper pencil grip.

Decorate the Letter: Apple Prints

Materials:
- 1 Apple (cut in half)
- Paint
- Fork or Popsicle Stick (to use as a handle)

Instructions:
- Cut an apple in half either horizontally or vertically (a horizontal cut will create a star shape with the seeds, but a vertical cut will help the print look more like the shape of an apple).
- Stick a fork or popsicle stick into the skin side of the apple to create a handle.
- Either dip the apple into a shallow plate of paint or brush paint onto the apple with a paint brush.
- "Stamp" the apple onto the blank A template.
- Once dry, cut the letter A out and glue it to a piece of construction paper.
- Title the paper "A is for Apple Prints".

Alternate Activity: Decorate the A template with apple or airplane stickers.

Letter Craft: A is for Alligator

Cut out each of the pieces and assemble them onto a blank piece of paper.
- Glue the green "A" down to a piece of construction paper.
- Glue the white triangles to form teeth in the mouth.
- Glue the eyes onto the top right side of the "A".
- Write "A is for Alligator" at the top of the page or use the provided label.

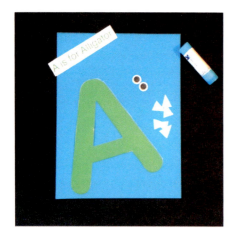

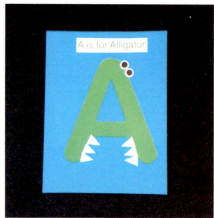

Snack/Food Ideas:

Apple, Apricot, Avocado, Acorn Squash

Musical Instrument:

Accordion

Other Activities:

Make paper airplanes.
Once the airplanes are made, you could have a contest to see which ones fly farther. This activity can be extended to compare and contrast the airplanes. Did different designs or airplane size effect the length the airplanes flew?

Make Apple Hand Pies.
- 1 package refrigerated pie crust
- 1 can apple pie filling
- 1 TBSP butter, melted
- cinnamon
- sugar

Allow pie crust to come to room temperate. Unroll pie crust and cut into small circles using a glass or cookie cutter. Place a spoonful of pie filling onto one half of the pie crust (the apples may need to be cut smaller to fit in the hand pie). Fold crust over and seal by pressing a fork around the outer edge. Cut three small slits in the top of the pie. Repeat until all circles have been filled. Place on a greased or parchment paper lined baking sheet. Brush each pie with melted butter and sprinkle with cinnamon sugar mixture. Bake at 425 degrees for 10-12 min. Enjoy!
(Two crusts and about half a 21oz can of filling will make 12-14 pies.)

A is for Alligator

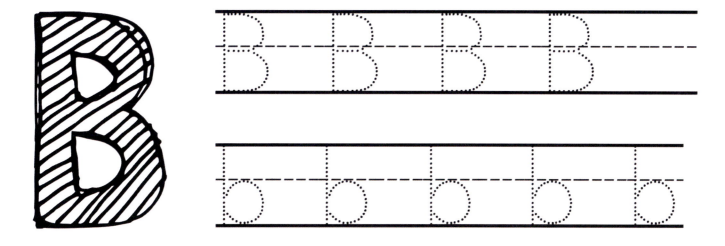

Letter Introduction:

Talk with your child about the letter "B" and the sound that the letter makes (it says "buh"). Help your child think of different objects that start with the letter B (basketball, balloon, banana, bear, bumblebee, bird, boat, bread, bubbles, butterfly, bicycle). You could look through books, pointing out objects that start with B or cut pictures from magazines and make a "B collage" together.

Also talk about how the letter is formed. Have your child trace over the letters provided above with his/her finger and then with a pencil or crayon. Try to encourage proper pencil grip.

Decorate the Letter: Bubble Prints

Materials:
- Bubbles and Bubble Wands
- Food Coloring
- Medicine Cups
- Tape

Instructions:
- Mix bubble solution and 1-2 drops of liquid food coloring in several small cups.
- Tape your letter template to a vertical surface (preferably outdoors).
- Have you child dip a bubble wand into the solution and blow bubbles onto the letter B template. When the bubbles pop, a spot of color should remain. Repeat with the different colors.
- Once dry, cut out the letter and glue it to a piece of construction paper.
- Title the paper "B is for Bubble Prints".
- If it's windy, you can lay the paper on a flat surface inside and blow the bubbles downward.

Alternate Activity: Decorate the B with buttons, or color it blue.

Letter Craft: B is for Bear

Cut out each of the pieces and assemble them onto a blank piece of paper.
- Glue the brown "B" down to a piece of construction paper.
- Glue the ears at the top of the "B".
- Glue the eyes, nose, hands, and feet down.
- Write "B is for Bear" at the top of the paper or use the provided label.

  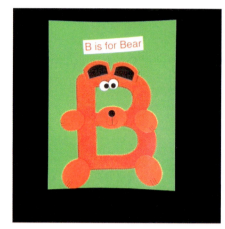

Snack/ Food Ideas:

Bananas, Banana Bread

Musical Instrument:

Banjo, Bells, Bagpipe

Other Activities:

Go on a bike ride.

Make a bird feeder.
Punch two holes in the top of an empty toilet paper roll to tie string through (to hang from the tree).
Spread a thin layer of peanut butter on the toilet paper roll.
Place birdseed on a plate and roll the cardboard tube through the seed.
Hang in a tree and enjoy watching the birds!

Make a banana bread.

1 cup sugar	1 cup mashed bananas (2-3 bananas)	1/2 tsp salt
1/2 cup butter	1 tsp vanilla	2 cups flour
2 eggs	1 tsp baking soda	1/2 cup pecans

Cream the butter and sugar together.
Add the eggs, bananas, and vanilla, and mix well.
Add baking soda, salt, flour, and pecans. Stir until just combined.
Pour into a greased loaf pan.
Bake at 350 degrees for about an hour (or until a toothpick inserted in the center comes out clean).

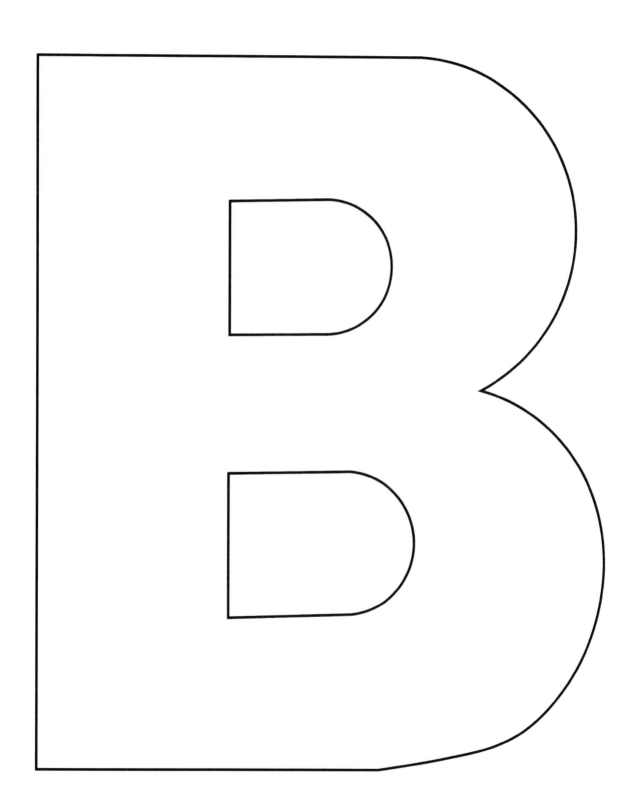

B is for Bear

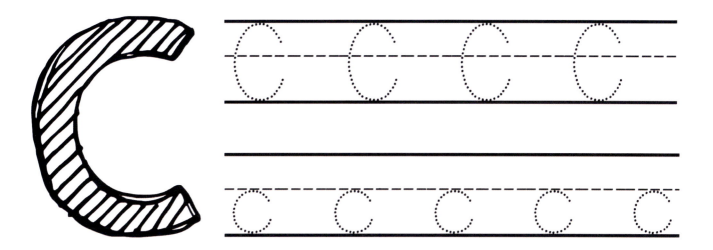

Letter Introduction:

Talk with your child about the letter "C" and the sounds that the letter makes (it says "kuh" and "sss"). Help your child think of different objects that start with the letter C (carrot, car, cupcake, corn, caterpillar, cow, centipede, centimeter). You could look through books, pointing out objects that start with C or cut pictures from magazines and make a "C collage" together.

Also talk about how the letter is formed. Have your child trace over the letters provided above with his/her finger and then with a pencil or crayon. Try to encourage proper pencil grip.

Decorate the Letter: Celery Prints

Materials:
- Celery
- Ink pads (paint would work fine too, but may not show as much detail)

Instructions:
- Break off one stalk of celery, and cut it into 3-4 pieces.
- Press the end of the celery into one ink pad, and "stamp" it onto the C template.
- Repeat with a clean piece of celery for each color.
- Once dry, cut the letter out and glue to a piece of construction paper.
- Title the paper "C is for Celery".

Alternate Activity: Color with C template with crayons.

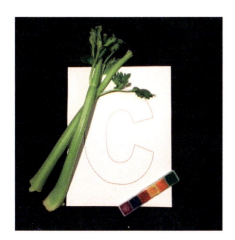

Letter Craft: C is for Cat

Cut out each of the pieces and assemble them onto a blank piece of paper.
- Glue the black "C" down to a piece of construction paper.
- Glue the ears and eyes at the top of the "C" and add the nose to center.
- Use a crayon to draw the whiskers and tail.
- Write "C is or Cat" at the top of the paper or use the provided label.

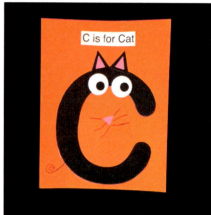

Snack/ Food Ideas:
Carrots, Cantaloupe, Cookies, Celery

Musical Instrument:
Clarinet, Cymbals, Cowbell

Other Activities:
Make and eat cookies.

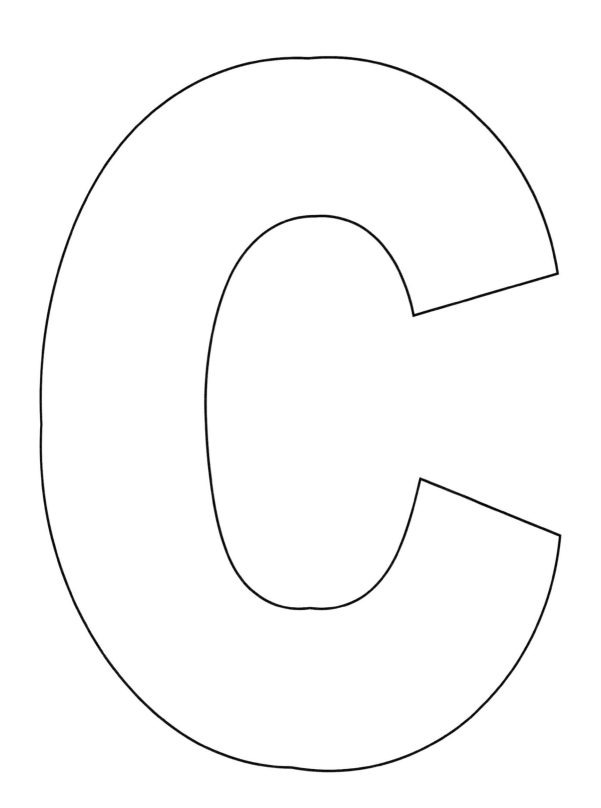

C is for Cat

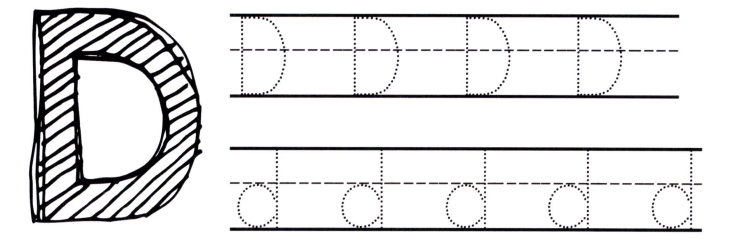

Letter Introduction:

Talk with your child about the letter "D" and the sound that the letter makes (it says "duh"). Help your child think of different objects that start with the letter D (duck, dinosaur, dog, drums, dolphin, dime). You could look through books, pointing out objects that start with D or cut pictures from magazines and make a "D collage" together.

Also talk about how the letter is formed. Have your child trace over the letters provided above with his/her finger and then with a pencil or crayon. Try to encourage proper pencil grip.

Decorate the Letter: Dot Paint

Materials:

- Dot Painters (Similar to a bingo dotter. Can be found at most craft stores.)
- 2 Dice (optional)

Instructions:

- Use dot painters to decorate the D template.

To make the activity more complex, you can use two dice to play a game as you paint.

- Tape a different color to each side of one die (use the colors of your dot painters).
- Roll both dice. (The one with colors will tell your child which color dot paint to use, and the one with numbers will tell your child how many dots to place on his/her letter.)
- Repeat the dice rolling until the letter is decorated to your child's liking.
- Once dry, cut the letter out and glue to a piece of construction paper.
- Title the paper "D is for Dot Paint".

Alternate Activity: Decorate the D template with stickers of objects that start with D.

Letter Craft: D is for Duck

Cut out each of the pieces and assemble them onto a blank piece of paper.
- Glue the orange star feet to the bottom of the "D" (on the back side of the letter).
- Glue the yellow "D" down to a piece of construction paper.
- Glue the circle head to the top of the "D". Add the eye and beak to the circle.
- Glue the wing to the left side of the "D". (You can use a yellow craft feather as well.
- Write "D is for Duck" at the top of the paper or use the provided label.

Snack/ Food Ideas:
Dates, Donuts

Musical Instrument:
Drums

Other Activities:
Play a game with dominoes.

Have a dance party.

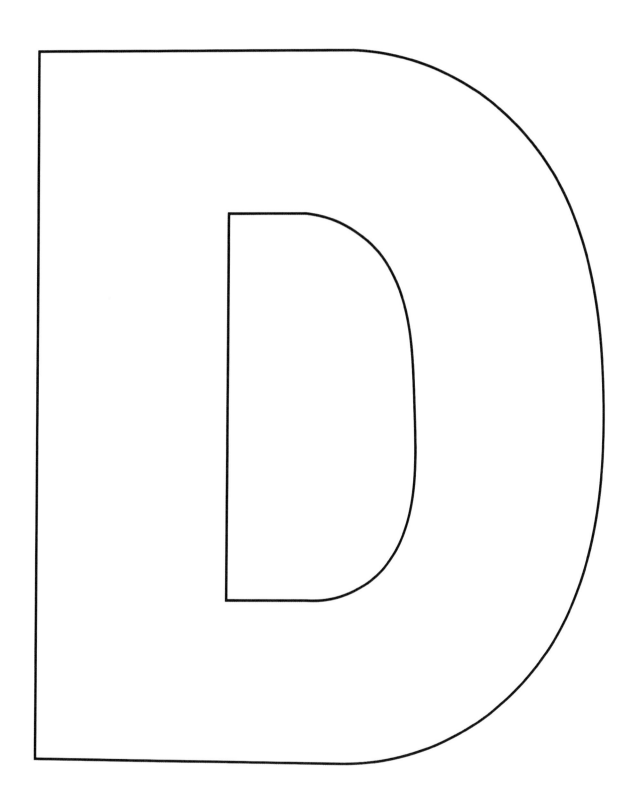

D is for Duck

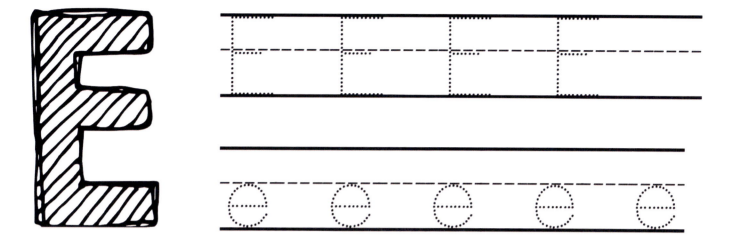

Letter Introduction:

Talk with your child about the letter "E" and the sounds that the letter makes (it says its name "e" and "eh"). Help your child think of different objects that start with the letter E (egg, elephant, elk, eagle, ear, eleven). You could look through books, pointing out objects that start with E or cut pictures from magazines and make an "E collage" together.

Also talk about how the letter is formed. Have your child trace over the letters provided above with his/her finger and then with a pencil or crayon. Try to encourage proper pencil grip.

Decorate the Letter: Easter Egg Prints

Materials:
- Easter Eggs (2-3)
- Paint

Instructions:
- Pour a few different colors of washable paint onto a paper plate or shallow dish.
- Open the plastic Easter eggs and use the open end to stamp the paint onto the egg.
- Once dry, cut the letter out and glue to a piece of construction paper.
- Title the paper "E is for Egg Prints".

Alternate Activity: Decorate the E template with googly eyes (found at most craft stores).

Letter Craft: E is for Elephant

Cut out each of the pieces and assemble them onto a blank piece of paper.
- Glue the grey "E" to a piece of construction paper.
- Glue the tusk to the backside of the trunk.
- Glue the trunk, ear, and eye to the "E".
- Draw a tail at the base of the "E".
- Write "E is for Elephant" at the top of the paper or use the provided label

Snack/ Food Ideas:
Eggs, Eggplant, Eclair, Enchiladas, Edamame

Musical Instrument:
Electric Guitar

Other Activities:
Dye hardboiled eggs.

E is for Elephant

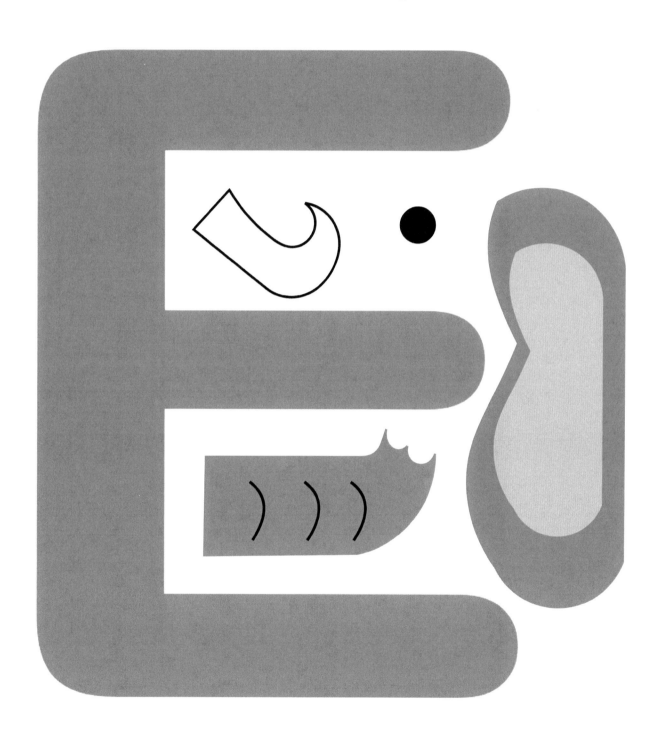

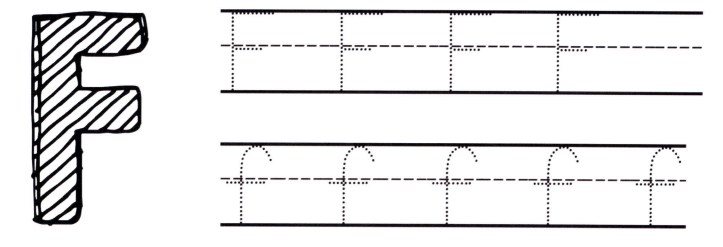

Letter Introduction:

Talk with your child about the letter "F" and the sound that the letter makes (it says "fuh"). Help your child think of different objects that start with the letter F (frog, fox, finger, flamingo, flower, football). You could look through books, pointing out objects that start with F or cut pictures from magazines and make a "F collage" together.

Also talk about how the letter is formed. Have your child trace over the letters provided above with his/her finger and then with a pencil or crayon. Try to encourage proper pencil grip.

Decorate the Letter: Fork Painting

Materials:
- Plastic Forks
- Paint

Instructions:
- Pour a few different colors of paint onto a paper plate or shallow dish.
- Place a plastic fork into each paint color.
- Have your child press the fork tines onto the F template to paint the F.
- Once dry, cut the letter out and glue to a piece of construction paper.
- Title the paper "F is for Fork".

Alternate Activity: Decorate the F with craft feathers or by finger painting.

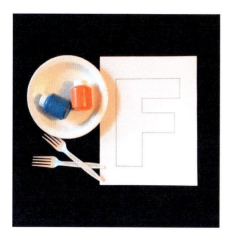

Letter Craft: F is for Fish

Materials:
- paint: white or blue (for bubbles) and green (for seaweed)

Instructions:
Cut out each of the pieces and assemble them onto a blank piece of paper.
- Glue the yellow "F" down to a piece of construction paper.
- Glue the fins, lips, and eye onto the "F".
- Use white or blue paint to finger paint a few bubbles above the fish mouth and green paint to paint seaweed next to the fish (or draw with a crayon).
- You can write "F is for Fish" at the top of the paper or use the provided label.

Snack/ Food Ideas:
Fish, French Toast

Musical Instrument:
Flute

Other Activities:
Make a flag.

Paint your child's fingernails.

Make a treat to take to the Firemen at your local firehouse. (It might be a good idea to call ahead to check your fire station's policy for visitors and treats.)

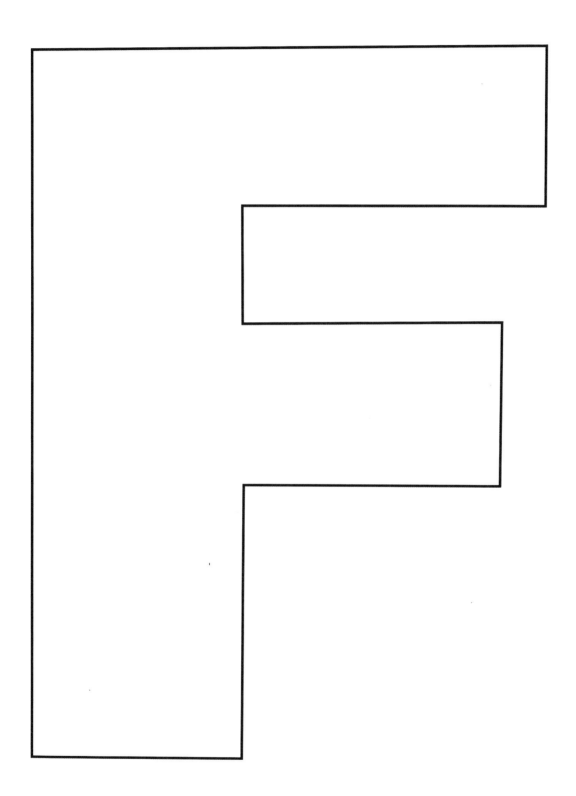

F is for Fish

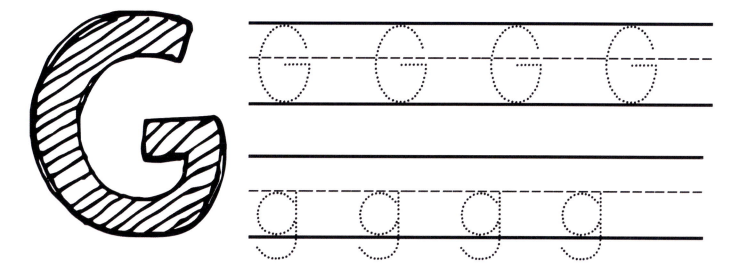

Letter Introduction:

Talk with your child about the letter "G" and the sound that the letter makes (it says "guh"). Help your child think of different objects that start with the letter G (girl, garden, goat, glove, grapes, green). You could look through books, pointing out objects that start with G or cut pictures from magazines and make a "G collage" together.

Also talk about how the letter is formed. Have your child trace over the letters provided above with his/her finger and then with a pencil or crayon. Try to encourage proper pencil grip.

Decorate the Letter: Golfball Painting

Materials:
- Golfball
- Paint (green)
- Casserole pan (disposable foil pans are a great option)
- Foil (optional for lining your pan)

Instructions:
- Pour paint onto a paper plate or shallow dish, and place a golfball in the paint.
- Place your template into a casserole pan.
- Place the golfball onto the paper and gently tilt your pan to cause the golfball to roll and "paint" your G template.
- Once dry, cut the letter out and glue to a piece of construction paper.
- Title the paper "G is for Golfball".

Alternate Activity: Color the G template green or glue green Easter grass onto the G template.

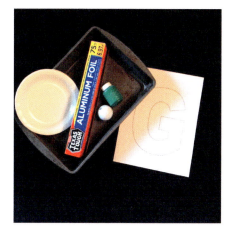

Letter Craft: G is for Gumball

Materials:
- dot paint, circle stickers, or pom poms (for "gumballs")

Instructions:
Cut out each of the pieces and assemble them onto a blank piece of paper.
- Glue the blue "G" down to a piece of construction paper.
- Glue down the red base and top, and add the grey rectangle door to the base.
- Use dot paint, crayons, different color circle stickers or pom poms to add "gumballs" to the blue "G".
- Write "G is for Gumball" at the top of the paper or use the provided label.

  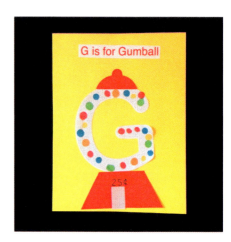

Snack/ Food Ideas:
Grapes, Grapefruit, Gingerbread

Musical Instrument:
Guitar

Other Activities:
Play putt putt golf.

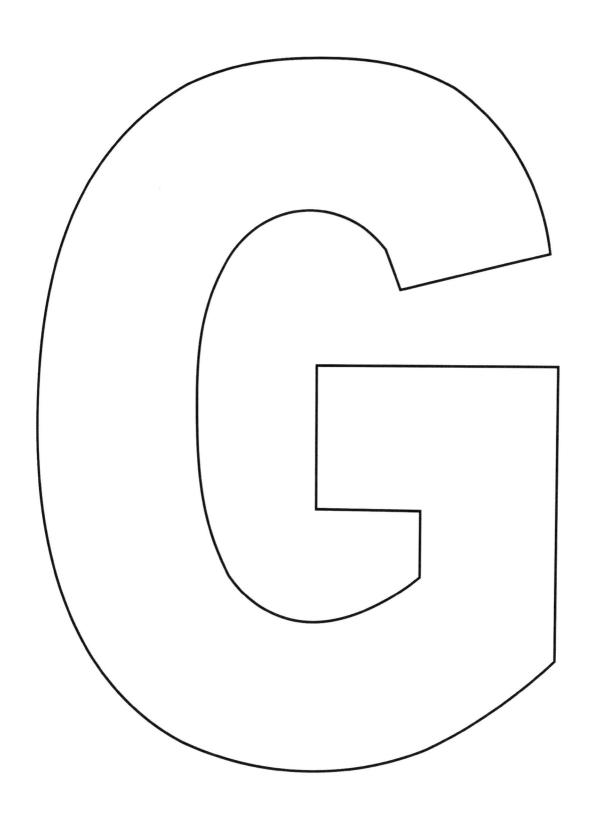

G is for Gumball

25¢

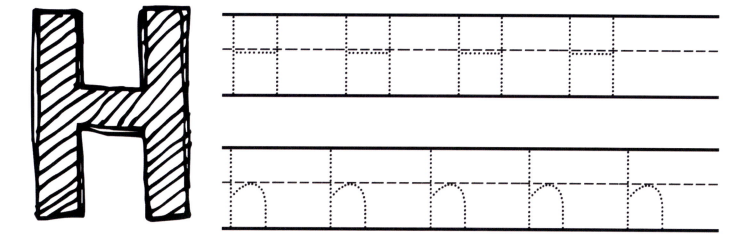

Letter Introduction:

Talk with your child about the letter "H" and the sound that the letter makes (it says "huh"). Help your child think of different objects that start with the letter H (heart, house, hammer, hat). You could look through books, pointing out objects that start with H or cut pictures from magazines and make a "H collage" together.

Also talk about how the letter is formed. Have your child trace over the letters provided above with his/her finger and then with a pencil or crayon. Try to encourage proper pencil grip.

Decorate the Letter: Highlighter

Materials:
- Highlighters (3-4 different colors)

Instructions:
- Set out several different colors of highlighters.
- Have your child color the H template with the highlighters.
- Once finished, cut the letter out and glue to a piece of construction paper.
- Title the paper "H is for Highlighter".

Alternate Activity: Decorate the H template with Hearts or Happy Faces.

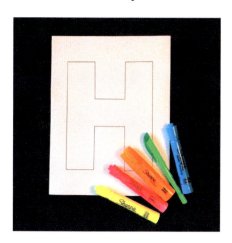
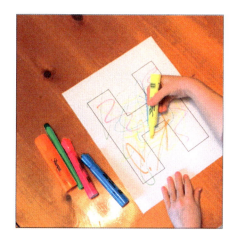

Letter Craft: H is for Horse

Cut out each of the pieces and assemble them onto a blank piece of paper.
- Glue the brown "H" down to a piece of construction paper.
- Glue down the head, ear, and hooves.
- Use scissors to snip the white lines on the mane and tail before gluing down. Be sure to put glue on just the solid part (not the snipped part).
- Write "H is for Horse" at the top of the paper or use the provided label.

 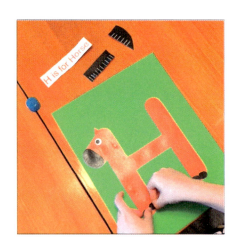 

Snack/ Food Ideas:

Hotdogs, Hamburgers, Honey, Hashbrowns

Musical Instrument:

Harp, Harmonica

Other Activities:

Play with a Hula Hoop.

Measure objects with your child's hand.
Compare the length of the different objects (Which one took the most hands? Least hands? Were any the same number of hands?)

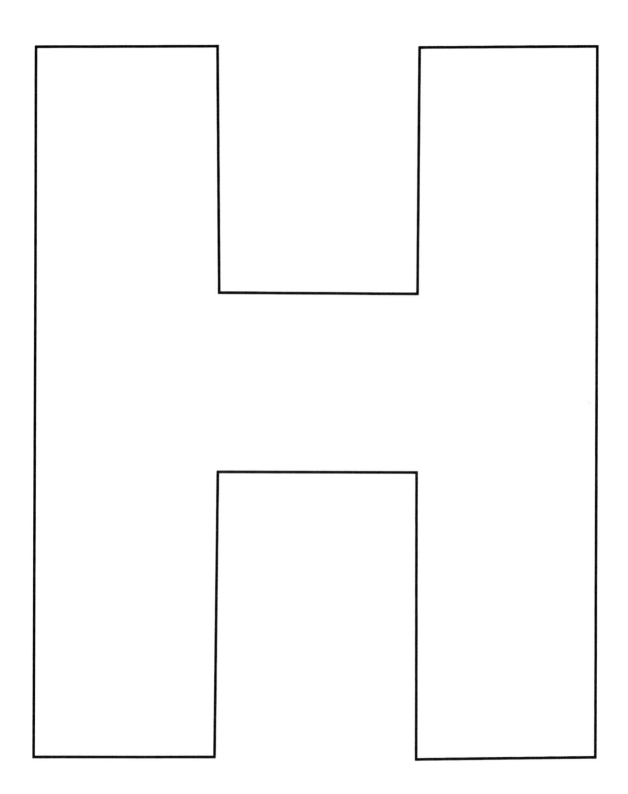

H is for Horse

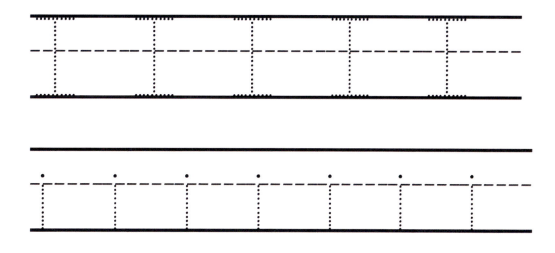

Letter Introduction:

Talk with your child about the letter "I" and the sounds that the letter makes (it says it's name "i" and "ih"). Help your child think of different objects that start with the letter I (ice cream, icicle, igloo, iguana). You could look through books, pointing out objects that start with I or cut pictures from magazines and make an "I collage" together.

Also talk about how the letter is formed. Have your child trace over the letters provided above with his/her finger and then with a pencil or crayon. Try to encourage proper pencil grip.

Decorate the Letter: Ice Painting

Materials:

- Ice cube tray or small paper cups
- Food Coloring
- Popsicle Sticks

Instructions:

- At least one day before doing this craft, fill an ice tray with water and 1-2 drops of food coloring.
- Place a popsicle stick into each water & color mixture and freeze. If the sticks are not staying straight, or are falling out, Cover the container with foil, and push the sticks through the foil. This should help hold the sticks in place. (small paper cups will work in place of an ice tray)
- Allow your child to "paint" the template with the melting ice. (Be careful not to paint too long because the template might rip if it gets too wet.)
- Once dry, cut the letter out, glue it to construction paper, and title it "I is for Ice Painting".

Alternate Activity: Decorate the I template with stickers of objects that start with I.

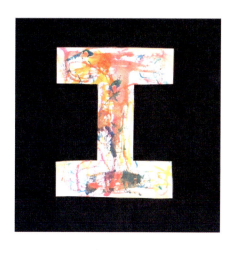

Letter Craft: I is for Iguana

Materials:
- red ribbon or crayon (for the iguana's tongue)
- tape

Instructions:
Cut out each of the pieces and assemble them onto a blank piece of paper.
- Glue the green "I" down to a piece of construction paper.
- Tape the ribbon to the back of the head. If you are using a red crayon, draw the tongue after the head has been glued down.
- Glue down the head to the top of the "I", and add the eyes and tail.
- Write "I is for Iguana" at the top of the paper or use the provided label.

  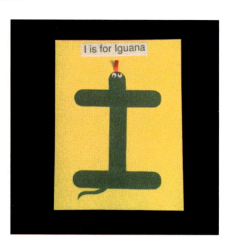

Snack/ Food Ideas:
Ice cream, Italian Food

Musical Instrument:
Instruments

Other Activities:
Make ice cream in a zip top bag.
- 1/2 cup half and half or milk
- 1 TBSP sugar
- 1 tsp vanilla
- sandwich and gallon zip top bags
- ice
- rock salt (optional)

Add the milk, sugar, and vanilla to small zip top bag, and seal the top. Place the ice, rock salt, and small zip top bag inside the large zip top bag. Seal the large bag. Shake or toss the bag for about 5 minutes or until the ice cream has formed. Gloves may be helpful if your child's hands get cold. Remove the small bag from the ice and enjoy your sweet treat either straight from the bag or scoop it into a bowl!

I is for Iguana

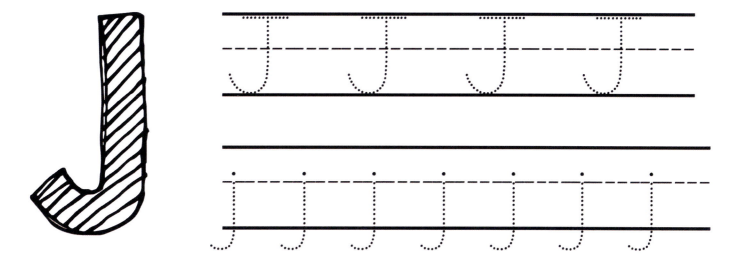

Letter Introduction:

Talk with your child about the letter "J" and the sound that the letter makes (it says "juh"). Help your child think of different objects that start with the letter J (juggle, juice, jack-o-lantern, jacket). You could look through books, pointing out objects that start with J or cut pictures from magazines and make a "J collage" together.

Also talk about how the letter is formed. Have your child trace over the letters provided above with his/her finger and then with a pencil or crayon. Try to encourage proper pencil grip.

Decorate the Letter: Jellybean Painting

Materials:
- Jellybeans
- Toothpicks
- Water

Instructions:
- Select different colors of jellybeans, and stick a toothpick into each one (to create a handle).
- Dip each jellybean into a shallow dish of water and then use it to "paint" the J template.
- Once dry, cut the letter out and glue to a piece of construction paper.
- Title the paper "J is for Jellybeans".

Alternate Activity: Stick "jewels" onto the J template (these can be found at most craft stores).

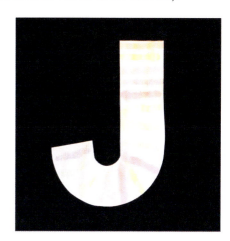

Letter Craft: J is for Jellyfish

Materials:
- Ribbon (for the jellyfish tentacles)

Instructions:
Cut out each of the pieces and assemble them onto a blank piece of paper.
- Cut 5-6 pieces of ribbon or string to use as tentacles.
- Glue the pink J down to a piece of construction paper.
- Tape ribbon or string to the back of the jellyfish body.
- Glue the body to the top of the J, and add the eyes
- Write "J is for Jellyfish" at the top of the paper or use the provided label.

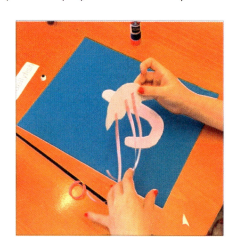

Snack/ Food Ideas:
Jellybeans, Juice Box, Jelly/Jam, Jambalaya, Jerky

Musical Instrument:
Jingle Bells, Jug (blow across the open top), Jazz

Other Activities:
Play a game of jacks.

Jump rope.

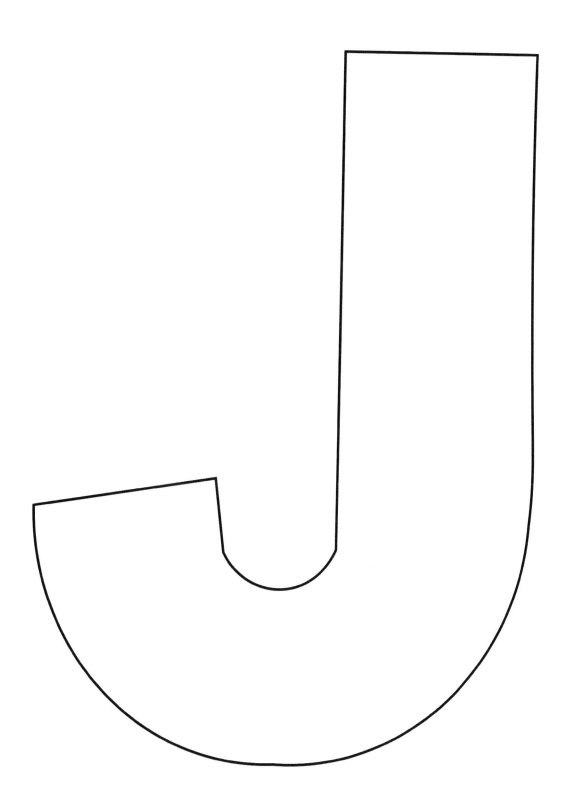

J is for Jellyfish

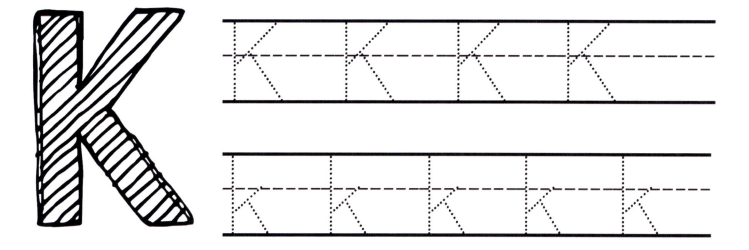

Letter Introduction:

Talk with your child about the letter "K" and the sound that the letter makes (it says "kuh"). Help your child think of different objects that start with the letter K (kangaroo, key, kite, kitten, koala). You could look through books, pointing out objects that start with K or cut pictures from magazines and make a "K collage" together.

Also talk about how the letter is formed. Have your child trace over the letters provided above with his/her finger and then with a pencil or crayon. Try to encourage proper pencil grip.

Decorate the Letter: Key Rubbing

Materials:
- Keys (of various sizes and shapes if possible)
- Crayons

Instructions:
- Place a key under the K template.
- Rub a crayon to color over the area with the key (the key outline should show up).
- Move the key to another spot, and rub another crayon over it.
- Once finished, cut the letter out and glue to a piece of construction paper.
- Title the paper "K is for Keys".

Alternate Activity: Decorate the K template with stickers of objects that start with the letter K.

Letter Craft: K is for Koala

Cut out each of the pieces and assemble them onto a blank piece of paper.
- Glue the brown K down to a piece of construction paper.
- Glue the koala onto the tree.
- Add the leaves onto the tree; feel free to draw in or cut and color more leaves if your child would like to.
- You can write "K is for Koala" at the top of the paper or use the provided label.

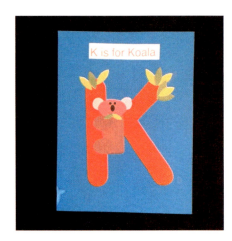

Snack/ Food Ideas:
Kiwi, Kabobs

Musical Instrument:
Kazoo

Other Activities:
Look through a kaleidoscope.

Fly a kite.

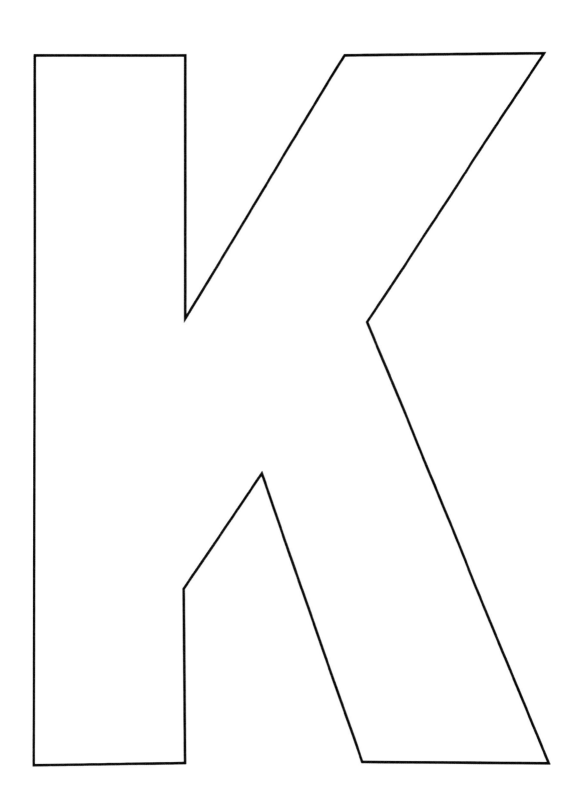

K is for Koala

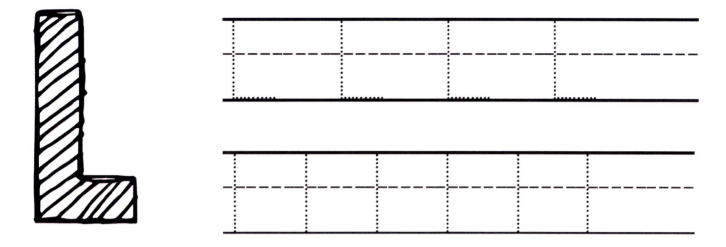

Letter Introduction:

Talk with your child about the letter "L" and the sound that the letter makes (it says "luh"). Help your child think of different objects that start with the letter L (ladder, lamp, leaf, ladybug, lips). You could look through books, pointing out objects that start with L or cut pictures from magazines and make a "L collage" together.

Also talk about how the letter is formed. Have your child trace over the letters provided above with his/her finger and then with a pencil or crayon. Try to encourage proper pencil grip.

Decorate the Letter: Leaf Painting

Materials:
- Leaves (of various sizes and shapes if possible)
- Paint

Instruction:
- Collect leaves from outside. Notice the different shapes, sizes, and colors.
- Pour a small amount of paint into a shallow dish or paper plate (green, orange, red, and yellow are nice colors to use as they resemble fall leaves).
- Use the leaves as paint brushes to paint the L template, or if the leaves are small, paint each leaf and stamp it onto the L template.
- Once dry, cut out the letter and glue it to a piece of construction paper.
- Write the title "L is for Leaf" at the top of the page.

Alternate Activity: Decorate the L template with leaf rubbings (similar to the letter K activity)

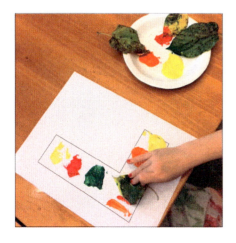

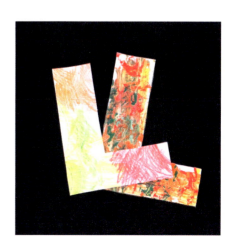

Letter Craft: L is for Lion

Cut out each of the pieces and assemble them onto a blank piece of paper.

- Tape or glue the legs to the back of the yellow "L"
- Glue the yellow "L" and legs to a piece of construction paper.
- Glue the nose to the left side of the "L".
- Glue the orange rectangles around the top and to the right of the "L" to resemble a mane, and then glue the ear in place.
- Draw in the eye and tail and glue the yellow teardrop piece to the end of the tail.
- Write "L is for Lion" at the top of the paper or use the provided label.

Snack/ Food Ideas:

Lasagna, Lettuce, Lemons

Musical Instrument:

Lyre

Other Activities:

Make lemonade.

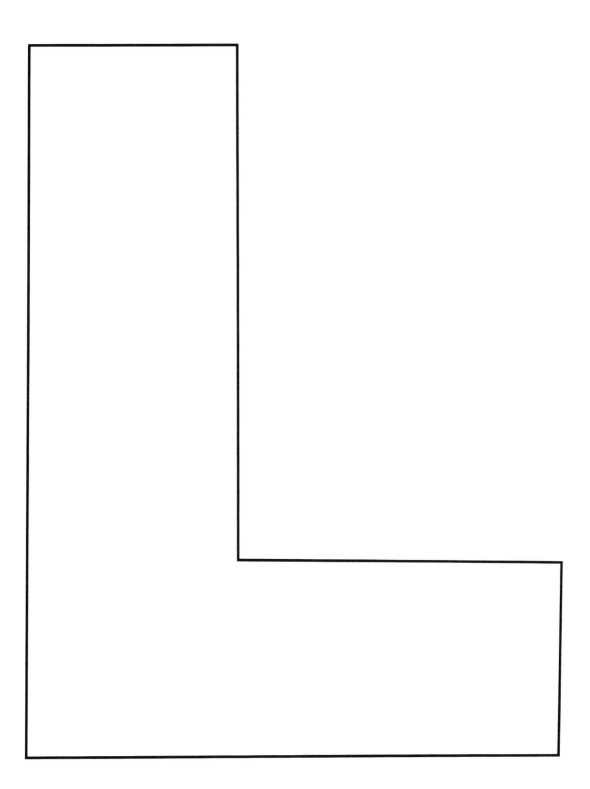

L is for Lion

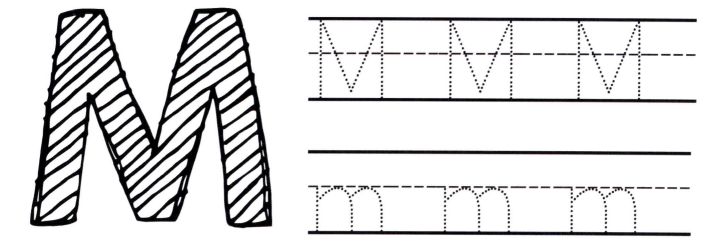

Letter Introduction:

Talk with your child about the letter "M" and the sound that the letter makes (it says "mmm"). Help your child think of different objects that start with the letter M (mailbox, milk, mittens, monster, monkey, moon, mustache). You could look through books, pointing out objects that start with M or cut pictures from magazines and make a "M collage" together.

Also talk about how the letter is formed. Have your child trace over the letters provided above with his/her finger and then with a pencil or crayon. Try to encourage proper pencil grip.

Decorate the Letter: Marshmallow Painting

Materials:
- Marshmallows
- Paint

Instructions:
- Pour a small amount of paint into a shallow dish or paper plate (use 3-4 different colors).
- Dip the marshmallow into the paint and then use it as a brush to paint the M template. (It may be easier and less messy if you first place a toothpick into the marshmallow to use as a handle.)
- Once dry, cut out the letter and glue it to a piece of construction paper.
- Write the title "M is for Marshmallow Painting" at the top of the page.

Alternate Activity: Color the M template with Markers.

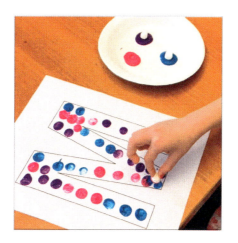

Letter Craft: M is for Mouse

Cut out each of the pieces and assemble them onto a blank piece of paper.

- Glue the grey M down to a piece of construction paper.
- Glue the ears, eyes, and nose in place.
- Draw whiskers on each side of the nose.
- Write "M is for Mouse" at the top of the paper or use the provided label.

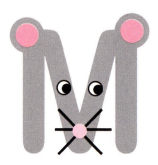

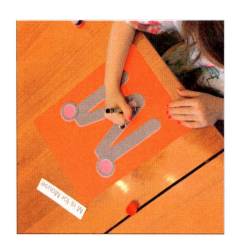

Snack/ Food Ideas:

Milk, Milkshake, Meatballs, Muffins, Mushrooms

Musical Instrument:

Maraca

Other Activities:

Make Maracas.

- Fill an Easter egg with dry rice or beans, and tape closed.
- Place the egg between two plastic spoons, and tape around the outside of the spoons.
- Decorate however your child desires (paint or stickers would probably work best).

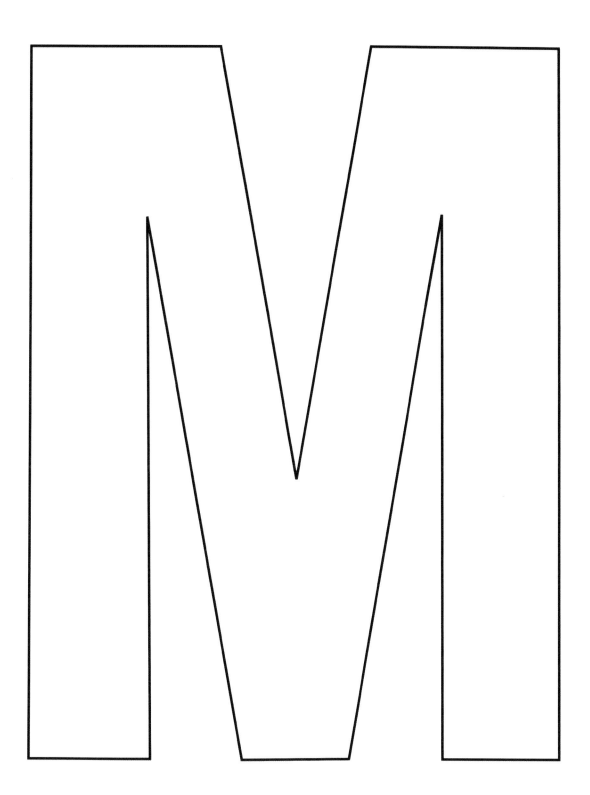

M is for Mouse

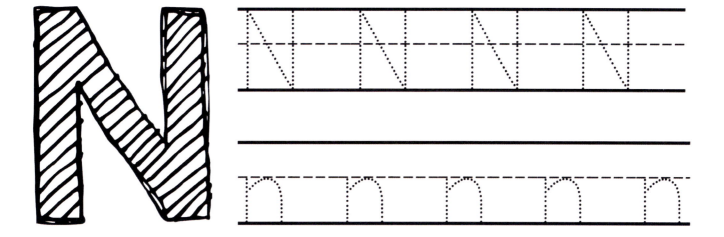

Letter Introduction:

Talk with your child about the letter "N" and the sound that the letter makes (it says "nuh"). Help your child think of different objects that start with the letter N (nail, needle, nest, net, nose, night, ninja, numbers). You could look through books, pointing out objects that start with N or cut pictures from magazines and make a "N collage" together.

Also talk about how the letter is formed. Have your child trace over the letters provided above with his/her finger and then with a pencil or crayon. Try to encourage proper pencil grip.

Decorate the Letter: Noodle Painting

Materials:
- Spaghetti Noodles
- Paint

Instructions:
- Boil spaghetti noodles until al dente.
- Pour a few different colors of paint into paper bowls and place a noodle in each paint color.
- Use the noodles to "paint" the N template.
- Once dry, cut out the letter and glue it to a piece of construction paper.
- Write the title "N is for Noodle Painting" at the top of the page.

Alternate Activity: Decorate the N template with pieces of newspaper.

Letter Craft: N is for Nest

Cut out each of the pieces and assemble them onto a blank piece of paper.
- Glue the brown N down to a piece of construction paper.
- Glue the small brown rectangles down to create a nest in the base of the N, and place the eggs in the nest.
- Build the bird and glue it to the top of the N. A craft feather can be used in place of the light blue wing if desired.
- Write "N is for Nest" at the top of the paper or use the provided label.

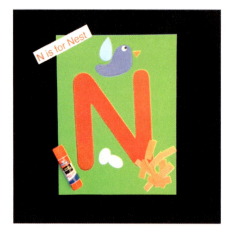  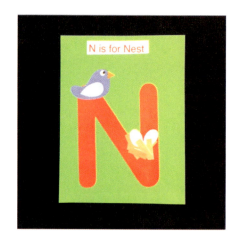

Snack/ Food Ideas:
Noodles, Nuts, Nachos

Musical Instrument:
Nose Flute

Other Activities:
Make a Noodle Necklace.

This can simply be done by taking tube shaped noodles and placing them on string or yarn. When choosing your noodles, be sure to choose ones that have openings large enough to easily string the noodles. Another fun activity is to first dye your noodles different colors! This is a quick and easy activity your child will likely enjoy helping with.

To dye your noodles, follow the instructions below:
- Noodles
- Rubbing Alcohol
- Food Coloring
- Zip Top Bags
- Wax Paper (optional)

Place noodles in several different zip top bags (about 1 cup per bag should be fine depending how many noodles you want to make). Pour about 1 TBSP rubbing alcohol into each bag. Put a few drops of color into each bag, and shake the noodles around. If you want a deeper color, add a few more drops of food coloring. Once the noodles are colored to your liking, pour the noodles out onto wax paper or a clean baking sheet. They will need to air dye for an hour or so. Once dry, create noodle necklaces and pictures! Store the noodles in an airtight container or bag for future use.
*Note: These are not safe to cook and eat due to the use of rubbing alcohol.

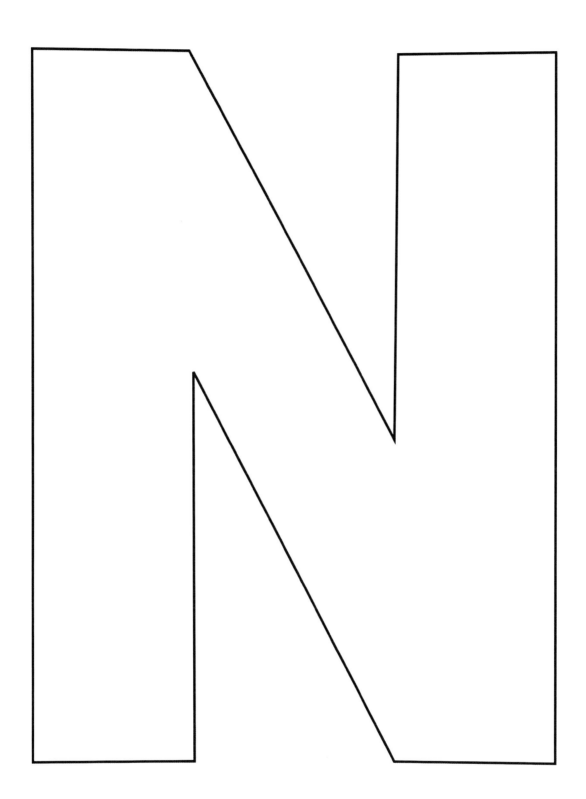

N is for Nest

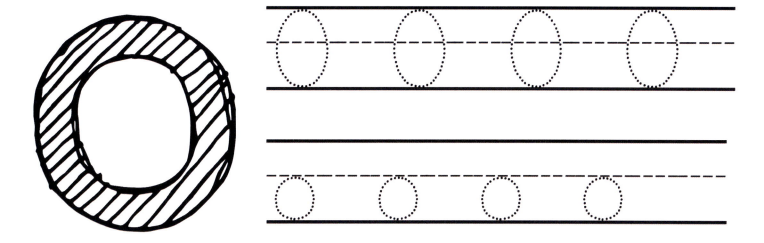

Letter Introduction:

Talk with your child about the letter "O" and the sound that the letter makes (it says "ah" and it's name "o"). Help your child think of different objects that start with the letter O (octopus, ostrich, oval). You could look through books, pointing out objects that start with O or cut pictures from magazines and make an "O collage" together.

Also talk about how the letter is formed. Have your child trace over the letters provided above with his/her finger and then with a pencil or crayon. Try to encourage proper pencil grip.

Decorate the Letter: Okra Stamping

Materials:
- Okra
- ink pad

Instructions:
- Cut the stem end off the okra.
- Press the end of the okra onto a stamp pad.
- Stamp the okra onto the O template.
- Once dry, cut out the letter and glue it to a piece of construction paper.
- Write the title "O is for Okra" at the top.

Alternate Activity: Paint or color the O template orange.

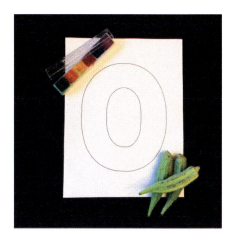

Letter Craft: (O is for Owl)

Cut out each of the pieces and assemble them onto a blank piece of paper.
- Glue the brown O down onto a piece of construction paper.
- Glue the small brown "triangles" at the top along with the eyes and beak. Finish the owl with the wings and legs.
- Write "O is for Owl" at the top of the paper or use the provided label.

Snack/ Food Ideas:

Oranges, Orange Juice, Okra, Olives

Musical Instrument:

Oboe, Organ

Other Activities:

Make fresh squeezed orange juice.

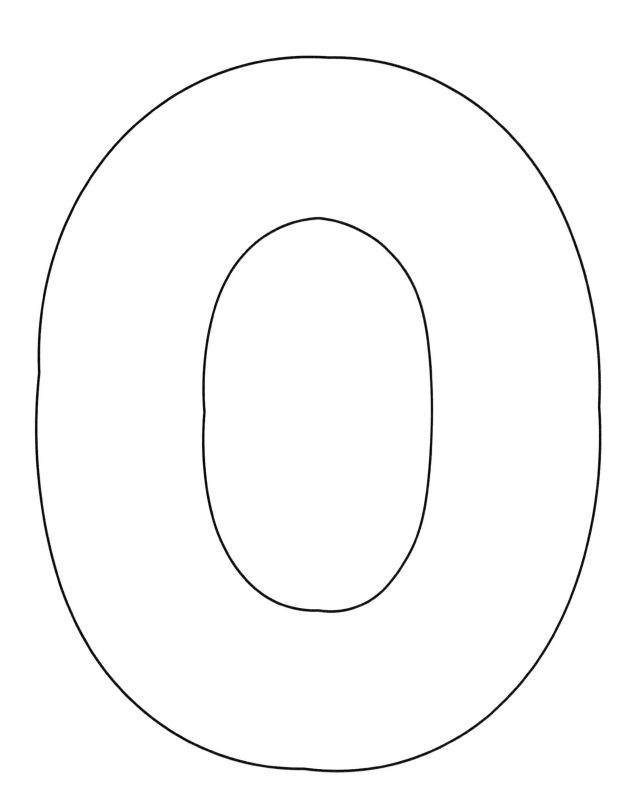

O is for Owl

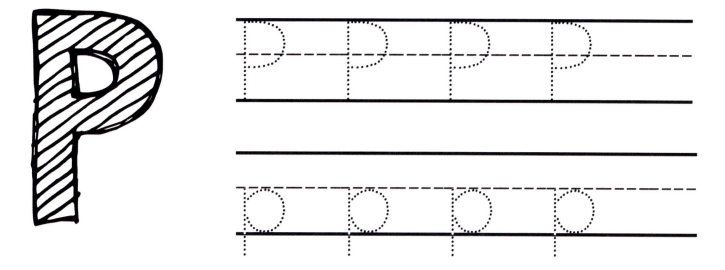

Letter Introduction:

Talk with your child about the letter "P" and the sound that the letter makes (it says"puh"). Help your child think of different objects that start with the letter P (pig, pancake, penguin, pumpkin). You could look through books, pointing out objects that start with P or cut pictures from magazines and make a "P collage" together.

Also talk about how the letter is formed. Have your child trace over the letters provided above with his/her finger and then with a pencil or crayon. Try to encourage proper pencil grip.

Decorate the Letter: Pencil Polk-a-dots

Materials:

- Pencil
- Paint (Use pink and purple paint if possible to extend the letter "P" theme.)

Instructions:

- Pour paint into a small plate or or shallow dish.
- Dip the eraser end of the pencil into paint and then dot it onto the template to create "polk-a-dots".
- Once dry, cut out the letter and glue it to a piece of construction paper.
- Write the title "P is for Polk-a-Dots" at the top of the page.

Alternate Activity: Paint or color the P template pink or purple or use a potato to make potato prints.

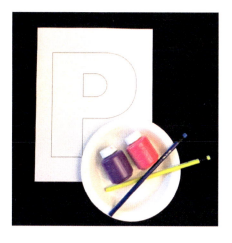
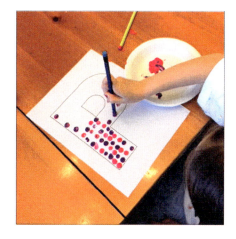

Letter Craft: P is for Peacock

Cut out each of the pieces and assemble them onto a blank piece of paper.

- Glue the feathers and legs to the back of the blue P. (Start with the center feather and then fan the rest out across the top half of the "p".)
- Glue the P and feathers to a piece of construction paper.
- Finish your peacock with the small head feather and beak.
- Write "P is for Peacock" at the top of the paper or use the provided label.

  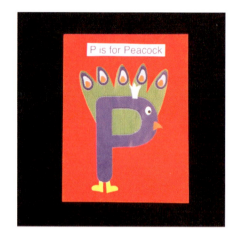

Snack/ Food Ideas:

Pepperoni Pizza, Pancakes, Popcorn, Pretzels

Musical Instrument:

Piano

Other Activities:

Do a puzzle together.

Go on a picnic.

Make play-dough:
- 2 cups flour
- 2 TBSP vegetable oil
- 1/2 cup salt
- 2 TBSP cream of tartar (a dry powder, found with cooking seasonings)
- 1 1/2 cups boiling water
- liquid food coloring

Mix flour, salt, cream of tartar, and oil together in a large mixing bowl. Measure the boiling water into a glass measuring cup, and add a few drops of food coloring to the water. Add the colored water to the flour mixture. Stir until the it becomes sticky. Allow the dough to cool slightly. Once cool enough to touch, knead the dough for several minutes (in the bowl or on a flat floured surface) until it is no longer sticky. If it remains sticky, add a little more flour in until the consistency is right. Play!
Store in an airtight container or plastic bag.

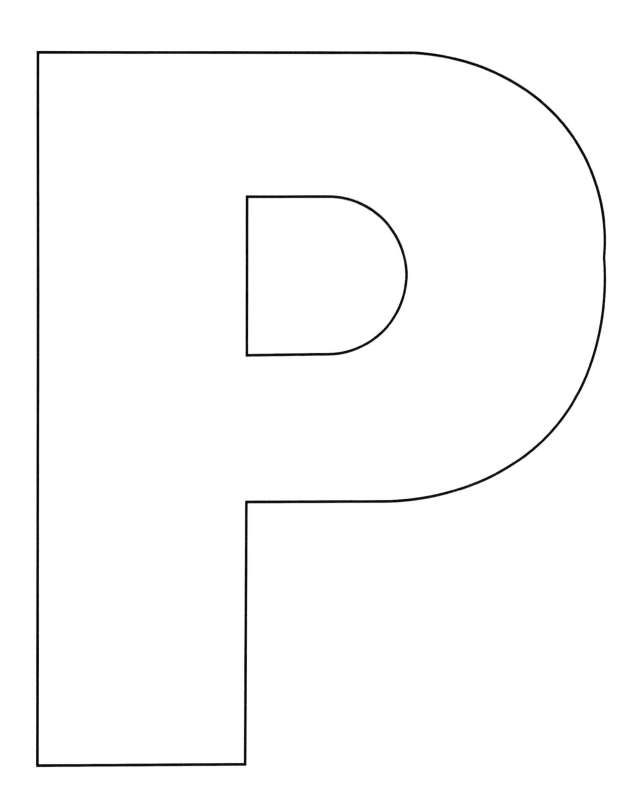

P is for Peacock

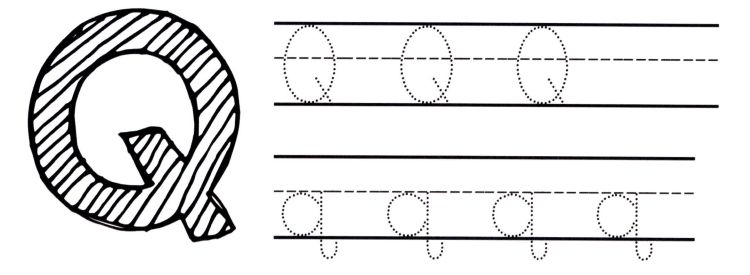

Letter Introduction:

Talk with your child about the letter "Q" and the sound that the letter makes (it says"kwuh"). Help your child think of different objects that start with the letter Q (queen, quarter, quilt, question mark). You could look through books, pointing out objects that start with Q or cut pictures from magazines and make a "Q collage" together.

Also talk about how the letter is formed. Have your child trace over the letters provided above with his/her finger and then with a pencil or crayon. Try to encourage proper pencil grip.

Decorate the Letter: Quilt

Materials:

- Scraps of fabric cut into 1 inch squares (40 - 50 squares)
- Glue stick

Instructions:

- Cut out the letter Q.
- Spread a small amount of glue onto one section of the Q, and cover with 1 inch fabric scraps. Repeat this process until the Q is completely covered.
- Once dry, trim the fabric around the Q and glue to a piece of construction paper.
- Write "Q is for Quilt" at the top of the page.

Alternate Activity: Use Q-tips to paint the Q template.

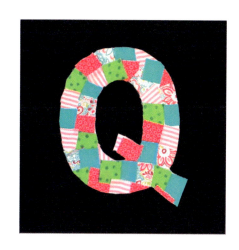

Letter Craft: Q is for Queen

Cut out each of the pieces and assemble them onto a blank piece of paper.
- Glue the tan Q down to a piece of construction paper.
- Glue the crown to the top of the Q. Decorate the crown with the provided paper jewels, or use stick on plastic jewels from your local craft store.
- Use the eyes and lips provided or draw your own to create the face of the queen.
- Write "Q is for Queen" at the top of the paper or use the provided label.

Snack/ Food Ideas:
Quesadillas, Queso, Quiche

Musical Instrument:
Quartet

Other Activities:
Make a crown and dress up like a queen!

Study different quilt styles.

Measure the length of different items with quarters. (Compare measurements… Which item was the most quarters long? Which needed to least quarters to measure the length? Were any items the same?)

Q is for Queen

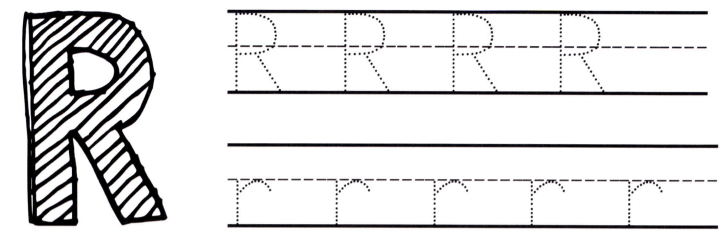

Letter Introduction:

Talk with your child about the letter "R" and the sound that the letter makes (it says "err"). Help your child think of different objects that start with the letter R (rainbow, ring, rock, robot, rocket). You could look through books, pointing out objects that start with R or cut pictures from magazines and make a "R collage" together.

Also talk about how the letter is formed. Have your child trace over the letters provided above with his/her finger and then with a pencil or crayon. Try to encourage proper pencil grip.

Decorate the Letter: Rainbow Painting

Materials:
- Pencil
- Ruler
- Paint, crayons, or markers (red, orange, yellow, green, blue, indigo, violet)

Instructions:
- Divide the R template into 7 horizontal sections (each about 1 inch thick) using a ruler to measure and draw a straight line.
- Have your child paint each section a color of the rainbow. I suggest dotting a little red paint in the first section, and having them spread it around between the pencil lines. Then repeat for each color (red, orange, yellow, green, blue, indigo, violet). If using crayons or markers, the adult might outline each section with the correct color, and then have the child color in each section.
- Once dry, cut out the letter and glue it to a piece of construction paper.
- Write the title "R is for Rainbow" at the top of the page.

Alternate Activity: Paint or color the R template red.

Letter Craft: R is for Rabbit

Cut out each of the pieces and assemble them onto a blank piece of paper.
- Glue the grey R down to a piece of construction paper.
- Glue the ears, eyes, and nose down.
- Draw whiskers and a mouth. A cotton ball tail can be added as well if you like.
- Write "R is for Rabbit" at the top of the paper or use the provided label.

Snack/ Food Ideas:
Rice, Raisins, Raspberries, Radishes

Musical Instrument:
Recorder, Rainstick

Other Activities:
Learn about recycling.

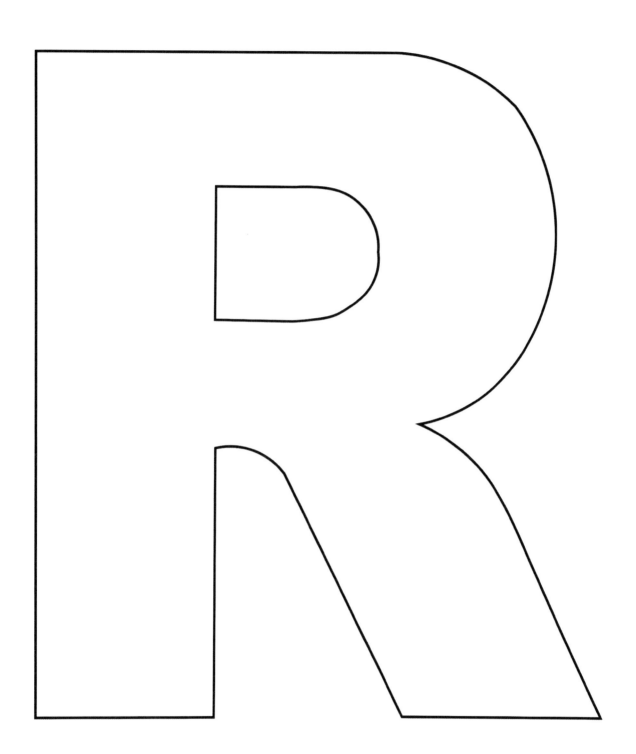

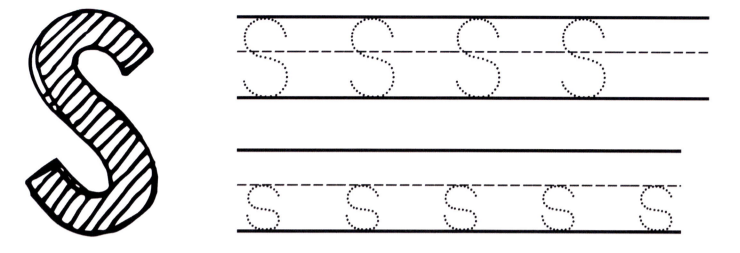

Letter Introduction:

Talk with your child about the letter "S" and the sound that the letter makes (it says "sss"). Help your child think of different objects that start with the letter S (swing, slide, socks, spoon, superhero). You could look through books, pointing out objects that start with S or cut pictures from magazines and make a "S collage" together.

Also talk about how the letter is formed. Have your child trace over the letters provided above with his/her finger and then with a pencil or crayon. Try to encourage proper pencil grip.

Decorate the Letter: Star Stickers or Stamps

Materials:
- Star Stamp or Star Stickers (star stickers should be easily found at most craft or grocery stores)

Instructions:
- Decorate the S template with Stars.
- You could also draw stars for your child to trace or color in.
- Cut out the letter and glue it to a piece of construction paper.
- Write the title "S is for Stars" at the top of the page.

Alternate Activity: Cut out small squares of different colors to decorate the template.

Letter Craft: S is for Snake

Cut out each of the pieces and assemble them onto a blank piece of paper.
- Glue the green S down to a piece of construction paper.
- Glue the eyes and tongue to the S.
- Glue down the square scales (note that square and scale also start with s).
- Write "S is for Snake" at the top of the paper or use the provided label.

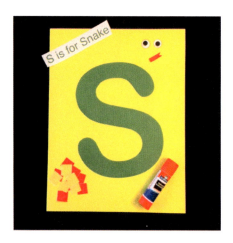 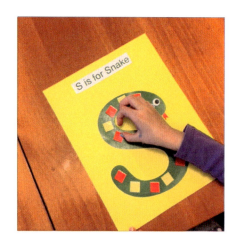 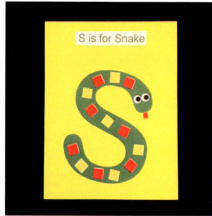

Snack/ Food Ideas:

Spaghetti, Spinach

Musical Instrument:

Saxophone, Sitar

Other Activities:

Ride a scooter.

Go swimming or to a splash pad.

Practice cutting with scissors.

Have a silly string fight outside.

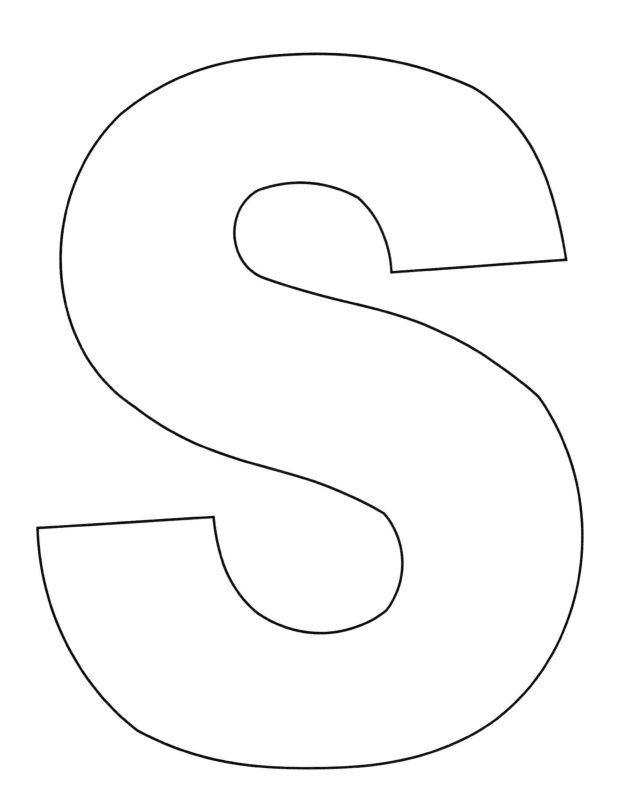

S is for Snake

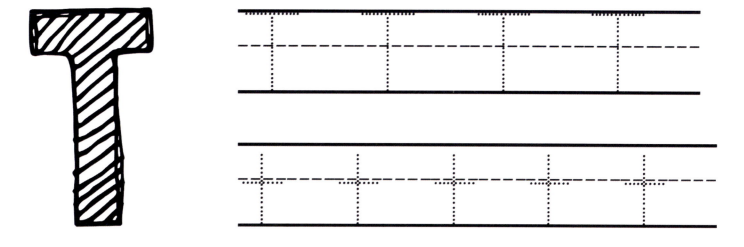

Letter Introduction:

Talk with your child about the letter "T" and the sound that the letter makes (it says "tuh"). Help your child think of different objects that start with the letter T (tractor, tree, turtle, turkey, triangle). You could look through books, pointing out objects that start with T or cut pictures from magazines and make a "T collage" together.

Also talk about how the letter is formed. Have your child trace over the letters provided above with his/her finger and then with a pencil or crayon. Try to encourage proper pencil grip.

Decorate the Letter: Toothbrush Painting

Materials:
- Toothbrush
- Paint

Instructions:
- Pour paint into a paper plate or shallow dish.
- Use an old toothbrush to paint the T template. Experiment with the different textures the toothbrush can make by smearing the paint, pressing the toothbrush up and down, or even running your thumb across the bristles to make it splatter (this step could get messy). Either throw the toothbrush away when finished, or save it for future painting projects.
- Once dry, cut out the letter and glue it to a piece of construction paper.
- Write the title "T is for Toothbrush" at the top of the page.

Alternate Activity: Cut out small triangles of different colors to decorate the template.

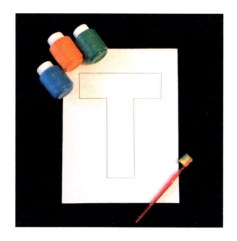

Letter Craft: T is for Tiger

Cut out each of the pieces and assemble them onto a blank piece of paper.
- Glue the orange T down to a piece of construction paper.
- Construct the face and draw in the whiskers and mouth. Glue it to the top of the T.
- Glue the tail down.
- Notice that the stripes are triangles (for letter T). Have your child count the triangles.
- Write "T is for Tiger" at the top of the paper or use the provided label.

  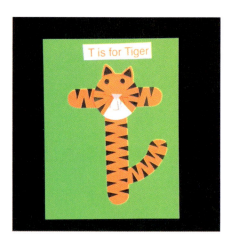

Snack/ Food Ideas:
Tortellini, Tomatoes, Toast, Tortilla

Musical Instrument:
Trumpet, Triangle, Tambourine

Other Activities:
Visit/ Ride a train.

Make a tambourine.
- 2 paper plates
- dry beans or rice
- stapler

Pour beans/ rice into one plate. Then place the other plate over the beans. Staple around the rim of the two plates until they are secure and no beans/rice can spill out. Decorate the plate with crayons, markers, or stickers.

T is for Tiger

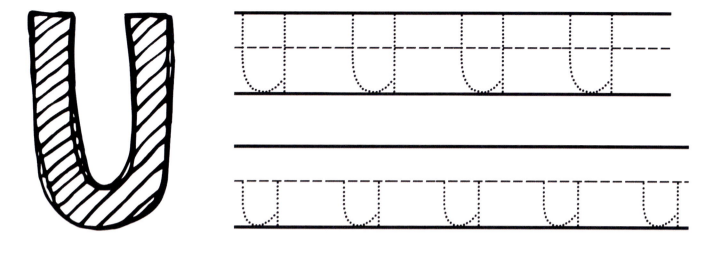

Letter Introduction:

Talk with your child about the letter "U" and the sound that the letter makes (it says it's name "u" and "uh"). Help your child think of different objects that start with the letter U (unique, unicorn, upside-down, umbrella). You could look through books, pointing out objects that start with U or cut pictures from magazines and make a "U collage" together.

Also talk about how the letter is formed. Have your child trace over the letters provided above with his/her finger and then with a pencil or crayon. Try to encourage proper pencil grip.

Decorate the Letter: Upside-down Coloring

Materials:
- Crayons
- Tape

Instructions:
- Tape the U template to the underside of a table top.
- Have your child color the template upside-down under the table.
- Once finished, cut out the letter and glue it to a piece of construction paper.
- Write the title "U is for Upside-down" at the top of the page.

Alternate Activity: Decorate the U template with family members finger prints (use an ink pad). Explain that each person's fingerprints are different and "unique" to them.

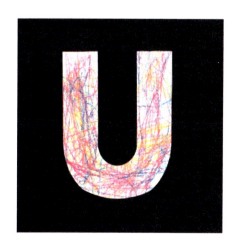

Letter Craft: U is for Unicorn

Cut out each of the pieces and assemble them onto a blank piece of paper.
- Glue the blue U down to a piece of construction paper.
- Attach the head, mane, tail, and horn to the U.
- Write "U is for Unicorn" at the top of the paper or use the provided label.

Snack/ Food Ideas:
Pineapple Upside-down Cake

Musical Instrument:
Ukulele

Other Activities:
Discuss what makes your child unique. Look beyond just physical characteristics that make them special. Talk about their interests, talents, and abilities as well. Have your child list things that make their family members unique as well.

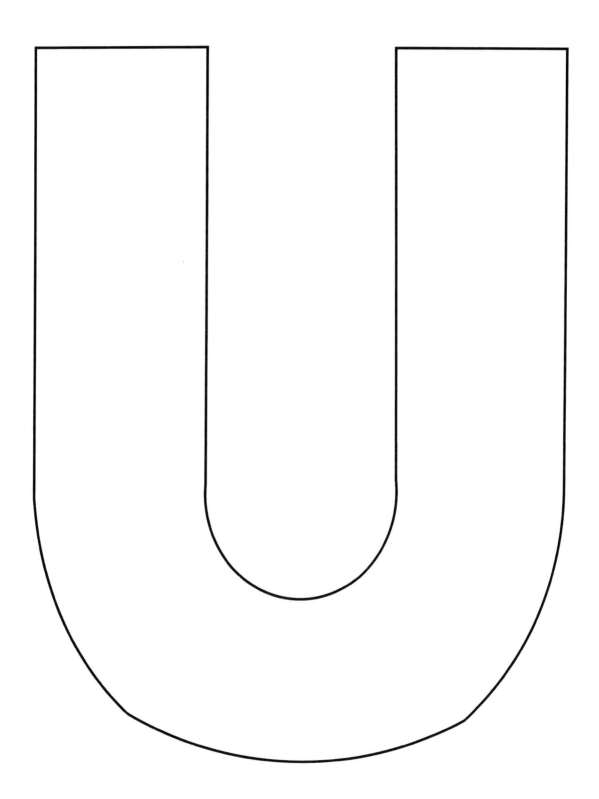

U is for Unicorn

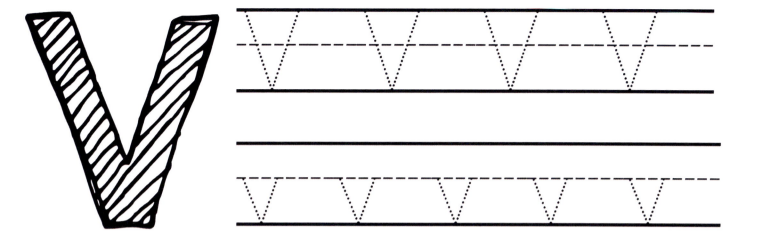

Letter Introduction:

Talk with your child about the letter "V" and the sound that the letter makes (it says "vuh"). Help your child think of different objects that start with the letter V (vest, vacuum, volcano, vulture). You could look through books, pointing out objects that start with V or cut pictures from magazines and make a "V collage" together.

Also talk about how the letter is formed. Have your child trace over the letters provided above with his/her finger and then with a pencil or crayon. Try to encourage proper pencil grip.

Decorate the Letter: Vehicle Painting

Materials:
- toy car (vehicle)
- paint (violet if possible to extend the "V" theme)

Instructions:
- Pour a small amount of paint onto a paper plate.
- Using a small toy car (vehicle), drive the wheels through paint and then drive the vehicle across the V template. Have your child say "vroom" as they paint to practice the "v" sound.
- Once dry, cut out the letter and glue it to a piece of construction paper.
- Write the title "V is for Vehicle" at the top of the page.

Alternate Activity: Color/Paint the V template violet, or use stickers of objects that start with V.

Letter Craft: V is for Vase

Cut out each of the pieces and assemble them onto a blank piece of paper.
- Glue the tan V down to a piece of construction paper.
- Glue the flowers above the V, and draw a green stem for each flower.
- Draw or glue the leaves onto the stems.
- Write "V is for Vase" at the top of the paper or use the provided label.

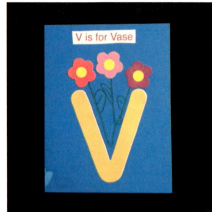

Snack/ Food Ideas:
Vegetables

Musical Instrument:
Violin, Viola

Other Activities:
Make a volcano.

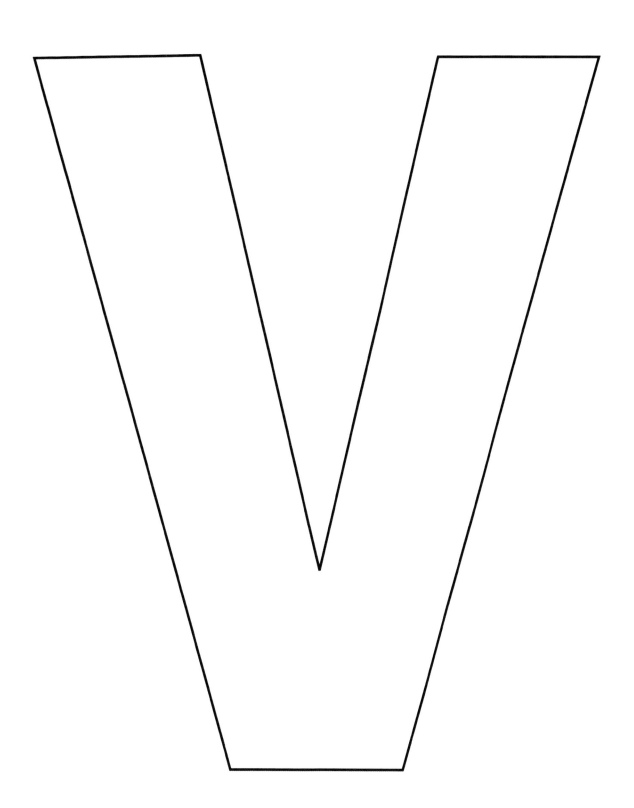

V is for Vase

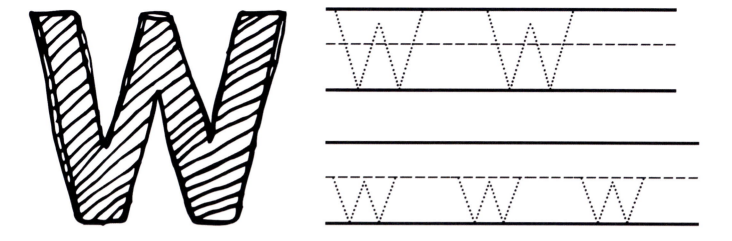

Letter Introduction:

Talk with your child about the letter "W" and the sound that the letter makes (it says "wuh"). Help your child think of different objects that start with the letter W (wagon, watch, whistle, winter). You could look through books, pointing out objects that start with W or cut pictures from magazines and make a "W collage" together.

Also talk about how the letter is formed. Have your child trace over the letters provided above with his/her finger and then with a pencil or crayon. Try to encourage proper pencil grip.

Decorate the Letter: Watercolor Painting

Mateirals:

- Watercolors
- Paint brush
- Water cup

Instructions:

- Use watercolors to paint the W template.
- Once dry, cut out the letter and glue it to a piece of construction paper.
- Write the title "W is for Watercolors" at the top of the page.

Alternate Activity: Use stickers of objects that start with W to decorate the template.

Letter Craft: W is for Walrus

Cut out each of the pieces and assemble them onto a blank piece of paper.

- Glue the dark brown head and light brown mouth to a piece of construction paper.
- Glue down the eyes, nose, and white "w" tusks.
- Draw in freckles and whiskers with a black crayon.
- Write "W is for Walrus" at the top of the paper or use the provided label.

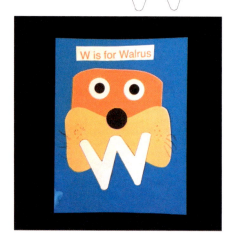

Snack/ Food Ideas:
Waffels, Watermelon

Musical Instrument:
Whistle, Wind Chime

Other Activities:
Have a water gun fight.

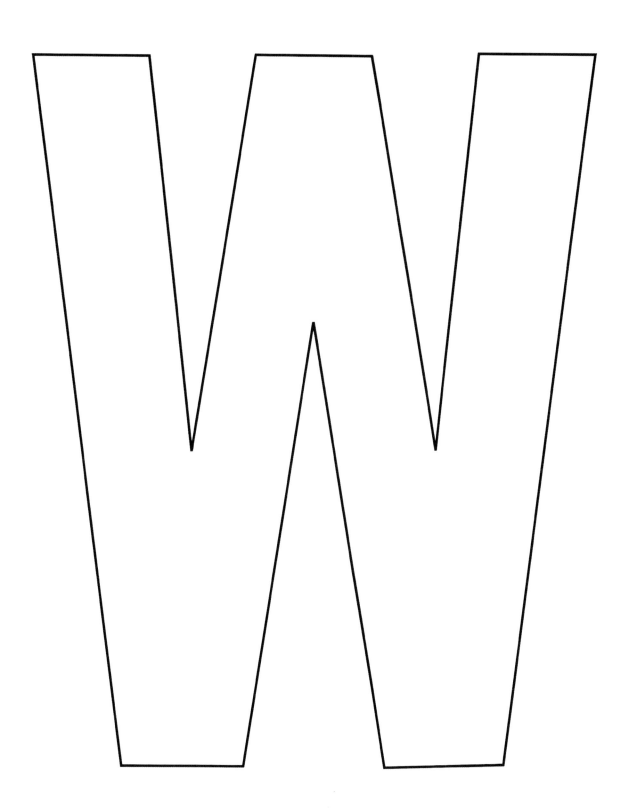

W is for Walrus

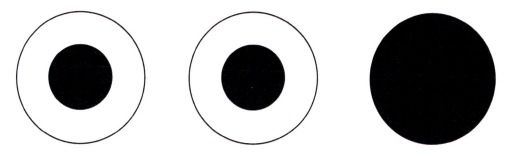

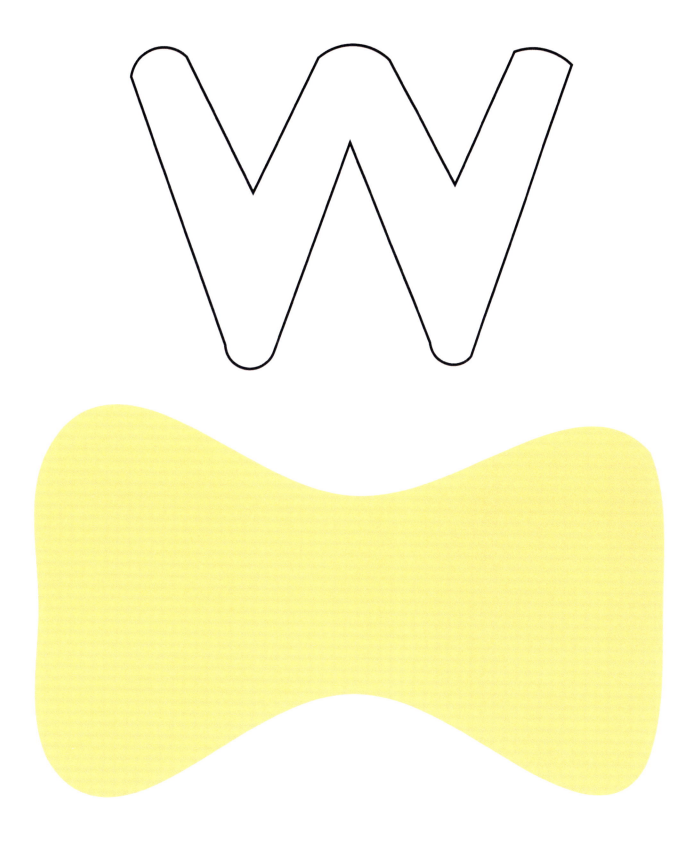

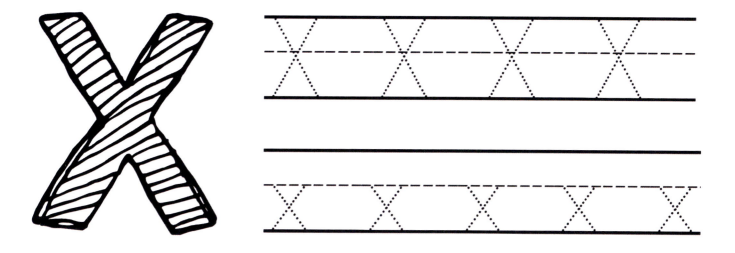

Letter Introduction:

Talk with your child about the letter "X" and the sound that the letter makes (it says "x", "zzz" when combined with a y, and "sss" at the end of a word). Help your child think of different objects that start with the letter X (x-ray, xylophone). Since not many words start with "X", you could also look for words that end with "X" (box, fox). You could look through books, pointing out objects that start with X or cut pictures from magazines and make a "X collage" together.

Also talk about how the letter is formed. Have your child trace over the letters provided above with his/her finger and then with a pencil or crayon. Try to encourage proper pencil grip.

Decorate the Letter: X-Ray

Materials:

- Black Crayon
- Scissors
- Glue Stick

Instructions:

- Cut the "bone" outlines out, so they don't get colored on by accident.
- Color the X template black.
- Glue the "bone" cut-outs to the X.
- Once finished, cut out the letter and glue it to a piece of construction paper.
- Write the title "X is for X-Ray" at the top of the page.

Alternate Activity: Use stickers of objects that start or end with X to decorate the template.

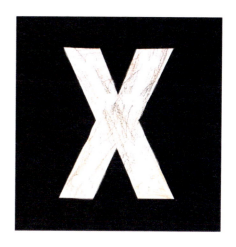

Letter Craft: X is or Xylophone

Cut out each of the pieces and assemble them onto a blank piece of paper.
- Glue the black X down to a piece of construction paper.
- Glue xylophone keys to the X (smallest to largest).
- Glue the mallet next to the xylophone. You can use the black circle that's provided or a black pom pom for the top of the mallet.
- Write "X is for Xylophone" at the top of the paper or use the provided label.

Snack/ Food Ideas:
Xigua (This is a melon commonly found in Africa. It has a hard green rind and a soft sweet pink interior with black seeds. It is also commonly known as watermelon.)

Musical Instrument:
Xylophone

Other Activities:
Create a treasure hunt with a map where "X" marks the spot of the hidden treasure.

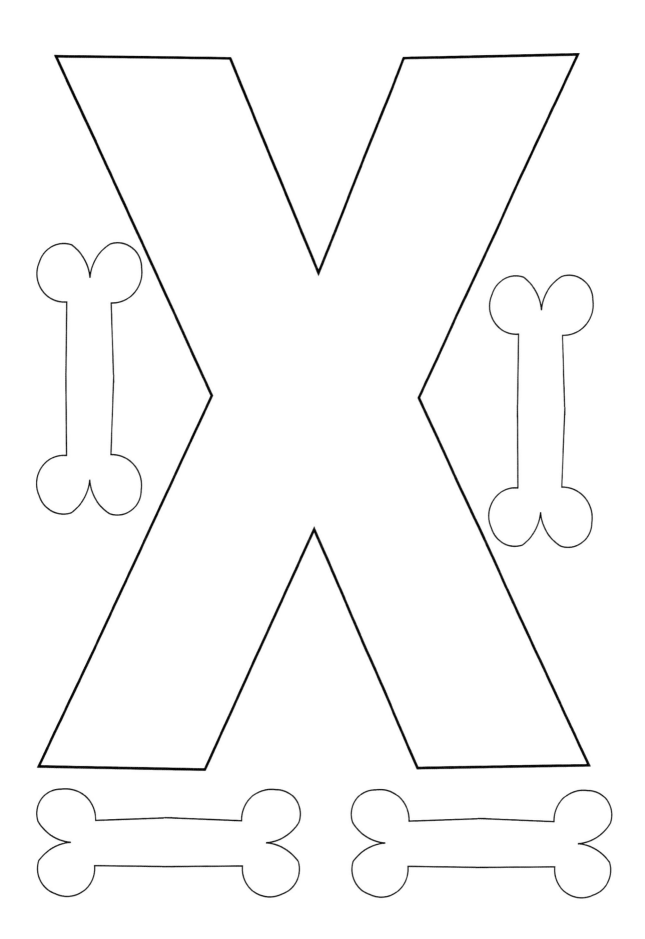

X is for Xylophone

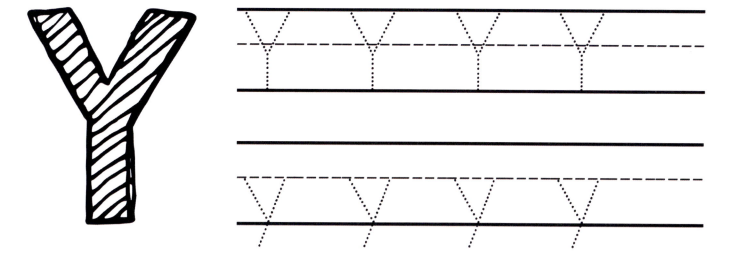

Letter Introduction:

Talk with your child about the letter "Y" and the sound that the letter makes (it says "yuh"). Help your child think of different objects that start with the letter Y (yarn, yo-yo, yellow). You could look through books, pointing out objects that start with Y or cut pictures from magazines and make a "Y collage" together.

Also talk about how the letter is formed. Have your child trace over the letters provided above with his/her finger and then with a pencil or crayon. Try to encourage proper pencil grip.

Decorate the Letter: Yarn Painting

Materials:
- Yarn
- Paint (consider using yellow paint to extend the "y" theme)

Instructions:
- Cut pieces of yarn at least 6 in.
- Pour paint to a plate or shallow dish.
- Dip the yarn into the paint and use it as a "paint brush" to paint the letter template.
- Once dry, cut out the letter and glue it to a piece of construction paper.
- Write the title "Y is for Yarn" at the top of the page.

Alternate Activity: Glue small pieces of yarn to the Y template or paint or color the Y yellow.

Letter Craft: Y is for Yak

Cut out each of the pieces and assemble them onto a blank piece of paper.
- Glue the brown Y down to a piece of construction paper.
- Glue down the horns, eyes, and snout.
- Draw in the nose and mouth with black and red crayon.
- Write "Y is for Yak" at the top of the paper or use the provided label.

Snack/ Food Ideas:
Yogurt, Yellow squash, Yuca root

Musical Instrument:
Yodeling

Other Activities:
Play with a yo-yo.

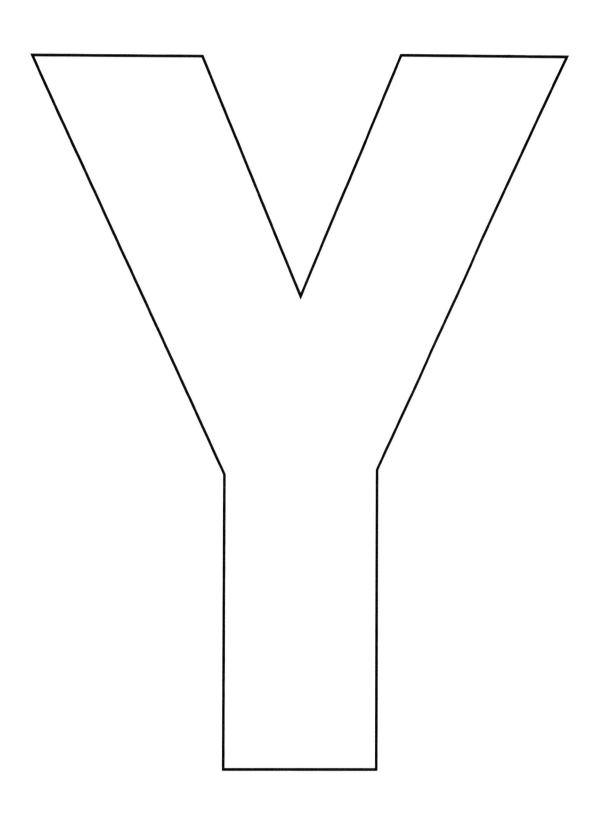

Y is for Yak

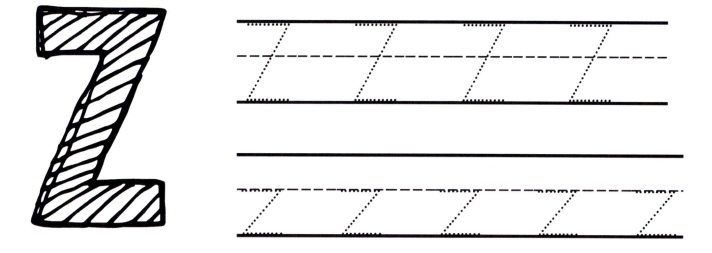

Letter Introduction:

Talk with your child about the letter "Z" and the sound that the letter makes (it says "zzz"). Help your child think of different objects that start with the letter Z (zoo, zipper, zero). You could look through books, pointing out objects that start with Z or cut pictures from magazines and make a "Z collage" together.

Also talk about how the letter is formed. Have your child trace over the letters provided above with his/her finger and then with a pencil or crayon. Try to encourage proper pencil grip.

Decorate the Letter: Z is for Zig-Zag

Materials:
- Ric-Rac Ribbon
- Liquid glue

Instructions:
- Glue down pieces of Ric-Rac Ribbon to decorate the Z template.
- Write the title "Z is for Zig-Zag" at the top of the page.

Alternate Activity: Have an adult draw zig-zags on the Z template in pencil or light color marker (like yellow). Then have the child trace over the zig-zags in a darker marker.

Letter Craft: Z is for Zebra

Cut out each of the pieces and assemble them onto a blank piece of paper.
- Glue the white Z down to a piece of construction paper.
- Glue the black stripes evenly throughout the Z.
- Glue the ear and nose to the Z.
- Draw in the eye, mouth, mane, and tail.
- Write "Z is for Zebra" at the top of the paper or use the provided label.

Zebra Stripe Alternative: Rather than gluing down the stripes. Place the plain white Z in a foil pan and roll a marble that's been dipped in black paint across the Z to make stripes (similar to the golfball painting activity from letter G).

Snack/ Food Ideas:
Zucchini, Ziti Pasta

Musical Instrument:
Zither

Other Activities:
Go to the zoo.
Do a letter scavenger hunt as you tour the zoo by finding animals and objects that start with each letter in the alphabet.

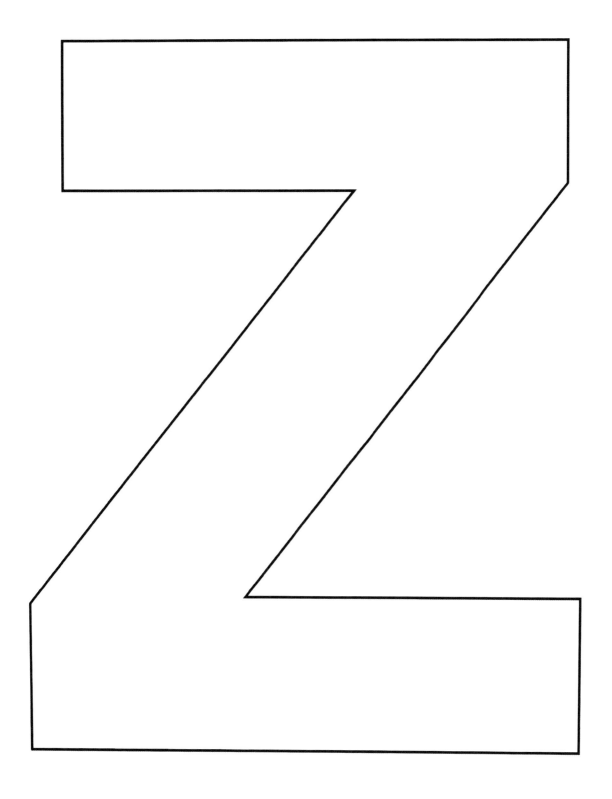

Z is for Zebra

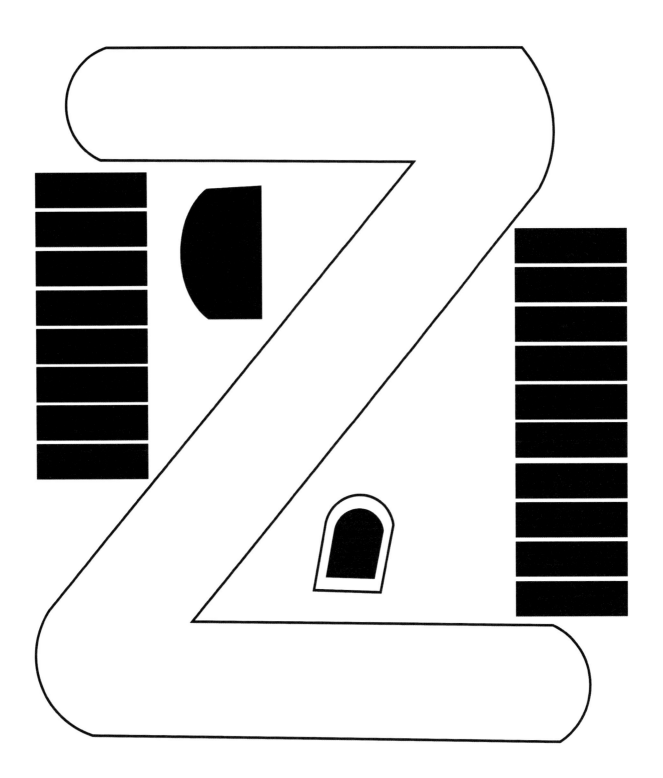

Made in the USA
Monee, IL
28 January 2021